EWAN
McGREGOR
FROM JUNKIE TO JEDI

BRIAN J. ROBB

Plexus, London

British Library Cataloguing in Publication Data

Robb, Brian J
    Ewan McGregor : from Junkie to Jedi
    1.McGregor, Ewan 2. Motion picture actors
    and actresses - Scotland - Biography
    I.Title
    791.4'3'028'092

ISBN 0 85965 276 9

Cover design by Philip Gambrill
Book design by Mitchell Associates
Printed in Great Britain by Jarrold Book Printing,
Thetford
Originated by PDQ Reprographic, Bungay, Suffolk

10 9 8 7 6 5 4 3 2 1

Acknowledgements
We would like to thank the following journalists,
newspapers and magazines whose interviews and
articles on Ewan were invaluable: *Edinburgh Evening
News*, January 3rd 1998, 'Uncle Denis teaches Ewan all he
knows' by Colin Somerville; *The Scotsman*, Oct 13th 1997,
'This boy's life so ordinary' by Brian Pendreigh; UK
Premiere, January 1995, 'Cameo: Ewan McGregor' by
Colette Maude; *Daily Record*, February 21st 1998, 'Ewan's
Tender Touch' & 'I'm the fan from Uncle' by Rick Fulton;
Time Out, February 7th 1996, 'The other side of the
tracks' by Tom Charity; *Sight & Sound*, February 1998,
'The boys are back in town' by Andrew O'Hagan &
Geoffrey McNab; *Empire*, March 1996, 'First Class
Return' by Caroline Westbrook; UK *Premiere*, March
1996, 'The anticipation is killing me' by Phillipa Bloom;
Neon, February 1998, 'Hey! Hey! We're the junkies!' by
Gareth Grundy; *Sight & Sound*, November 1996, 'Body
Talk' by Peter Greenaway; *Guardian Weekend*, August
13th 1994, 'Local hero in Hollywood' by Bob Flynn; *The
Face*, October 1997, 'Ewan and Cameron's Extraordinary
Adventure' by Charles Gant; *Empire*, November 1997,
'Caledonian Supernova' by Ian Nathan; *Sky*, November
1997, 'This One's Taken' by Sophie Wilson; *Details*,
November 1997, 'Ewan McGregor Straight Up' by Gavin
Edwards; *Total Film*, December 1997, 'Heavenly
Creatures' by Cam Winstanley & Dean Evans; *Neon*,
October 1997, 'The Scot Report' by Chris Heath; *Film
Review*, March 1998, 'The New Hope' by Marion Ross;
Edinburgh Evening News, July 8th 1998, 'Licensed to reel'
by Colin Somerville; *Edinburgh Evening News*, February
28th 1998, 'Anna's Mutual Friend' by Colin Somerville

Other publications consulted: *Sunday Times*, *The
Guardian*, *The Times*, *Time Out*, *You* Magazine, *The
Independent*, *Film Review*, *Eva*, *Elle*, *US* Magazine, *Time*,
Entertainment Weekly, *People*, *Sunday Life*, *InterVUE*, *Irish
Times*, *Miami Herald*, *PaperMag*, *W*

Press Notes for *Kavanagh QC* (ITV); *Family Style* (Ch4);
Being Human; *Shallow Grave*; *Blue Juice*; *The Pillow Book*;
Trainspotting; *Emma*; *Nightwatch*; *Brassed Off*; *The Serpent's
Kiss*; *A Life Less Ordinary*; *Velvet Goldmine*; *Star Wars: The
Phantom Menace* (official web site)

Our thanks are due to the following photographers,
libraries and film companies for supplying photographs:
Sasha Gusov whose photographs appear on p.1, 6, 18, 26,
27, 42, 71, 80, 90, 104 and 106; Armando Gallo/Retna,
Swirc/MPA/Retna, Steve Granitz/Retna, Jim
Cooper/Retna, Gavin Edwards/Retna; All
Action/O'Brien/Peters, Paul Smith/All Action; The
British Film Institute; the BBC; Colin McPherson; Press
Association; Alan Davidson; Alpha, Stefan Rousseau/PA
Photos, Steve Finn/Alpha, Randolph Caughie/Alpha,
John Leyton/Alpha, Dave Benett/Alpha; Gavin
Evans/Retna; London Magazine/Premiere/ Polygram
Film International; All Action/Polygram Film
International; Grampian Television; Marc
Guillamot/Film Four Distributors, Peter Mountain/Film
Four Distributors/Goldwyn Films Int Ltd; Granada
Films; Miramax Films International/Consolidated
Communications; J+M Entertainment; Polygram Film
International; Warner Brothers; Channel Four
Films/Figment Films/Glasgow Film Fund/Gramercy
Pictures/Polygram Filmed Entertainment; Skreba Films;
Channel Four Films; Channel Four Films/Figment
Films/Polygram Filmed Entertainment/The Noel Gay
Motion Picture Company/Haft
Entertainment/Matchmaker Films/Miramax Films;
Michael Obel/Dimension Films; Channel Four
Films/Miramax Films; the Studio Canal+/France 2
Cinema/President Films/Trinity/Berryer
Films/Nef/Red Parrot/Rose Price Battsek; Figment
Films/Polygram Filmed Entertainment/Channel Four
Films; Channel Four Films/Miramax
Films/Zenith/Single Cell Pictures/Killer
Films/Goldwyn Films/Newmarket Capital Group;
Granada Film Producution/Newmarket Capital;
Whistling Gypsy Production/Channel Four Films; BBC;
Ariel Productions for the BBC.

CONTENTS

CHAPTER 1

A LIFE LESS ORDINARY

THE FORCE would certainly appear to be with rising Scottish movie star Ewan McGregor. Cast as the young Obi Wan Kenobi in George Lucas's second *Star Wars* trilogy, McGregor is charged with the task of both filling the shoes of Sir Alec Guinness, who originated the role, and with ensuring that the most successful franchise in movie history enjoys a new lease of life for the new millennium.

Ewan McGregor is now a big name in Hollywood following a rise to fame over just a few years in a string of decidedly non-Hollywood film roles. From playing a cynical Edinburgh hack journalist in the low-budget macabre thriller *Shallow Grave* to becoming the poster boy for the drug culture in the phenomenally successful *Trainspotting*, McGregor's rise has been inexorable.

Ewan has carved a reputation as something of a cinematic workaholic. A total of fifteen feature films completed in less than five years is an astonishing feat by any standards. That these films should reveal him as an actor of uncanny natural abilities and wide audience appeal is even more startling.

It's perhaps surprising Ewan became an actor at all, as he originally wanted to be a rock singer. 'It's the idea of standing there in front of all those thousands of people. It's just you, it's your music, it's not about pretending to be somebody else,' he admitted. 'I don't have the guts, but I would like to know what that feels like. It's a fantasy, the rock'n'roll lifestyle. Because I've got a kid, I'm married and I've got a house, I can't do all that stuff.'

'I'd be happy if I could work with Danny [Boyle] forever.'

The nearest Ewan has got to playing out his rock'n'roll fantasy was on the big screen in Todd Haynes's seventies-set glam rock epic *Velvet Goldmine*. In real life, the would-be rock star never pursued his ambition beyond playing drums in a band during his teenage years. A huge fan of Brit-pop bad boys Oasis, he also managed to sing a few bars of one of the band's more obscure B-side tracks in a scene from *A Life Less Ordinary*.

The pathway to success for Ewan McGregor has been in his relationship with a creative trio. Producer Andrew Macdonald (the grandson of Emeric Pressburger, the acclaimed screenwriter and film-making partner of Michael Powell), writer and ex-doctor John Hodge and director Danny Boyle first cast Ewan in *Shallow Grave*, their low-budget debut assault on the period-costume-drama-dominated world of British film-making. Such was the bond between the star and the three talents behind the camera that they worked together again very quickly, with the lead roles in both *Trainspotting* and *A Life Less Ordinary* being tailored specifically for Ewan.

'I'd be happy if I could work with Danny [Boyle] forever,' Ewan has claimed of a relationship that was to be sorely tested. 'I'm never happier working with anyone else. He makes films the way I think they should be made, really . . . He gets my best work. I don't know how or why, but I'm not as good with anyone else.'

However, it was the surprise decision of George Lucas to cast Ewan as the young Obi Wan Kenobi for his trio of *Star Wars* prequels that secured his status as a worldwide star.

Ewan Gordon McGregor was born on 31 March 1971 in the small, quiet town of Crieff in Scotland's Perthshire. The town nestles in the foothills of the Grampian Highlands, about 60 miles north of the central urban belt of Glasgow and Edinburgh. The nearest conurbation of any size is the coastal town of Perth on the Firth of Tay to the east.

Ewan's mother, dark, wavy-haired Carol Diane McGregor, is a retired teacher who still lives in Perthshire and now serves as McGregor's personal assistant, while father James Charles

Stewart McGregor – just known as Jim – was for many years a physical education teacher and careers adviser at Morrison's Academy, the private school Ewan McGregor attended as a day pupil, along with his more academically inclined older brother Colin. He, too, is now retired.

Acting is in the family blood, because Ewan's mother's brother, Denis Lawson – McGregor's uncle – is a professional actor of note. As Ewan grew up in the mid-seventies, he was aware that his Uncle Denis was an unusual kind of man. Lawson himself knew that he'd chosen an unusual kind of profession, given his family's background.

'We lived in Crieff, which is a tiny, provincial, Perthshire market town with about 6000 people,' Lawson recalled of his early days. 'It was an odd place to be an actor. My grandfather used to entertain for hours on two glasses of sherry – but that's not quite the same thing.'

Lawson quickly saw that if he was to pursue his chosen career, staying in Crieff wasn't an option, even though he owes his drive to his family. 'My mum, Phyllis, is 75 and still runs a business in Crieff. She is a human dynamo. Our family are always on the go,' he has said.

For Ewan, his uncle's experience and achievements were a guiding light. He knew he wanted to be an actor from about the age of nine – and he knew he'd have to leave Crieff to do it – just as his uncle had done. 'Crieff was the kind of place that I eventually wanted to leave. That's nothing against the place itself, but there isn't a great acting industry in Crieff, so obviously I had to get out. It was really green. I used to rampage around forests and there was a big hill that we used to kick around on called the Knock. So, if I think about my childhood, I think about that: kicking around forests and riding horses and stuff like that. Kind of lads' stuff, because in the countryside you kind of go around in packs.'

Until he started to take his acting ambitions seriously, Ewan was a typical 1970s Scottish kid. The McGregor family lived in a good sized semi-detached house in Sauchie Terrace, in a less imposing part of a town dominated by Victorian stone villas. Here the young Ewan played on a toy tractor up and down Sauchie Terrace, or raced his childhood pal James Kerr in a pedal car. Shortly after going to Kerr's fifth birthday party, Ewan moved with his family to a three-bedroom home in Murray Drive, a somewhat more affluent area of the town.

The move did little to stifle his youthful enthusiasm. He was like any adventurous kid, getting into silly fights and heading off on wild adventures with his school pals, Malcolm Copland and Euan Sinclair. On one occasion his recklessness resulted in a trip to hospital and a scare for his parents. Racing downhill on his bike and playing the macho stunt rider, imagining himself to be Evel Knievel – who was all the rage at the time – Ewan tried to turn a corner without braking and ended up being treated for concussion in hospital after flying over the handlebars and into the road.

Shortly afterwards, he decided to run away from home. He left the house one afternoon, declaring himself fed up with everything and everyone. This was a half-hearted rebellion, as the would-be thespian had his mother make him a sandwich to run away with, and he took his dog along, too. Ewan didn't run off far. He headed up to the top of the Knock. It was on this tree-covered hill that he was found, snacking on his sandwich, sitting under a tree with his dog's leash tied to a branch.

In fact, Ewan was often to be found up at the Knock after school and at weekends, playing rough and tumble games with his friend Malcolm Copland, now a sales manager who still lives in Crieff. Ewan would muck out stables every weekend at the Crieff Hydro, simply for the chance to ride the horses. The summers Ewan spent playing in the countryside around Crieff were times he would remember with affection. 'You know, spending all day with your mates, with catapults and stuff, getting up to no good,' he recalled. 'It was great. I had a brilliant time.'

An event which would help shape his future happened when Ewan was six years old in 1977. He attended Sunday School regularly. Although his parents Jim and Carol were not particularly religious, they believed in making a wide range of knowledge and experience available to their children in order that they could make up their own minds about the world. For Ewan, Sunday School meant the chance to act in a play of the story about David and Goliath.

The Reverend Henry Tait, who retired in autumn 1997 from Crieff South Church, told *The Scotsman* that he wrote the part of David especially for Ewan, lifting the challenging dialogue directly from the Bible. He recalled that the young McGregor needed no encouragement or cajoling to perform. 'This child had a natural flair,' he recalls observing, presciently.

There was only one thing which could have held the aspiring actor back – he still couldn't read, despite his parents' work in education. His mother vividly remembers practising the role with him, reassuring the minister that his young leading actor would know it by the time of the performance. Young Ewan was also spotted practising his lines alone in the church hall, so seriously did he take the opportunity to appear on stage in front of his local community. Ewan was determined to get everything right. By the end of that process, he was word perfect. The Reverend Tait said that he noted in his diary that Ewan was 'outstandingly good' as David. Tait would be one of the first people Carol McGregor would tell when Ewan got his first big break as a professional actor.

Ewan and his friends also took great pride in their playground recreation of the fifties-set musical hit *Grease*. He and a mate would take turns each being Olivia Newton-John and John Travolta. 'One of us would be Olivia and another would be John. I was a very good Olivia Newton-John,' he admitted of an early play-acting role that really stretched his developing talents. 'I don't think there was any touching or kissing involved. We were just kids, you know. Obviously it helped to make me a sensitive and interested performer . . .'

He even claimed to have crossed his fingers for a year in the hope that Olivia Newton-John would happen to get lost in Crieff and stop off at his house, but instead had to make do with re-enacting 'You're The One That I Want' in the school playground.

Despite the amusement it had generated, the attractions of *Grease* soon palled. 'We moved on to the catapult stage, where we just used to fire catapults at girls on horses.' He and his friends built a den from ferns and twigs which, he claimed, 'the SAS would be proud of'. It was a place to hide after firing off a volley of missiles from their Black Widow catapults, made more deadly with tubular rubber elastic. It was not unusual for the gang to set out to hit old women and horses, something Ewan now reluctantly admits. 'It was a childish thing, I've got a deep love of horses – I'd never shoot one in the arse now.'

Ewan would play other parts off stage for his own amusement. As punk was making its mark on the British music scene of 1976-7, six-year-old Ewan McGregor was busy being Elvis Presley. 'I would spend a great deal of my time being Elvis because he was the best thing. 'I don't remember ever not knowing about him.'

Ewan used to entertain adults at parties thrown by his parents by singing 'Lonesome Tonight' and 'Love Me Tender', whilst imitating Presley's distinctive dance movements. This talent for rock'n'roll mimicry was to serve him well later in life. The real song that affected Ewan as a child, though, was the sentimental classic 'Old Shep'. 'I used to sit and weep to "Old Shep" over and over again, which made me the sensitive guy I am now,' he claimed, ironically. He has often drawn on the song to help him out in important emotional scenes in his acting life – or so he has claimed. 'Some people think about their sister being raped and stuff like that to get them in the mood,' he has said of other actor's approaches to playing intense emotional scenes, 'but I just listen to "Old Shep".'

'I would spend a great deal of my time being Elvis because he was the best thing.'

Another significant event for the six-year-old was the release of the film *Star Wars* in the UK in January 1978, following its astonishing American debut the previous year. Only a short time had passed between his turn on stage at Crieff South Church and a trip to the cinema to see his interestingly bohemian uncle, who had a featured part in the film.

Although young Ewan had a rough idea of what his uncle did for a living – he pretended to be other people, didn't he? – he had never actually seen him in a performance on film. Outside of the main stars, Denis Lawson turned out to be one of the few actors to appear in all three of the first *Star Wars* movies, playing the part of heroic X-Wing pilot Wedge Antilles. Seeing him 'was the most exciting thing that had happened in my life. It was a kind of double whammy: the movie threw me and so did he.'

It was to be the beginning of a life-long love affair with both acting and with the unique universe of *Star Wars* in particular. 'I remember later we had the first one on [video] tape and me and my friends knew every line, more or less. We'd be able to do the whole dialogue to *Star Wars*. I did a very

'I don't stand for anything, I don't see myself as a figurehead.'

Left: Ewan appearing on
Grampian Television's A
Touch of Music which his
father taped and used to
embarass him with in later life

'When I was fourteen I got thrown off a golf course for swearing. After every shot I would get really angry, screaming "Fuck!"

good Princess Leia in the playground. I wanted to be Carrie Fisher, with the Danish hair buns. She was one of my first crushes, you see. I had a really serious crush on her because she looked great.'

Subsequently Ewan became his uncle's biggest fan. 'Ewan used to come and see all the things I did,' Lawson told the *Edinburgh Evening News*. 'He picked up the acting vibes from me. I suppose I was very different from everyone else he knew.

To this day, nephew and uncle stay in close touch, living near each other in London. It was especially useful when it came to Ewan's turn to take on the *Star Wars* machine. 'Ewan and I have a very close relationship which I value enormously and I am also very fond of Colin [Ewan's older brother]. Ewan and I live within walking distance in London and, when we have the time and the energy, we go out and drink a lot and chat.'

For his part, Ewan credits his uncle with encouragement in his early years and for the fact that he had led by example. 'Denis helped me with my audition speeches when I started out,' he told the *Daily Record*. 'He has always been there to give me advice. His success is partly why I'm here. I've been watching him perform all my life and I love watching.'

Ewan recalled the visits Denis would make to the McGregors' house in Crieff. He would often turn up wearing a threadbare Afghan waistcoat and beads. 'I thought, who is this guy? He was really different, and then I suppose I developed this need to be different as well. It's probably still part of my character to this day, and I don't know where it comes from – I suppose some desperate lack somewhere.'

Ewan's developing acting ambitions, nurtured by parts in plays at school, did not at first block out his alternative dream of being a musician. 'I was quite musical at school. I've got French horn to grade 7, I did a couple of concertos, and I played in the school pipe band as a side drummer,' explained Ewan. He also played in a ceilidh band and in a pop band called Scarlet Pride, a name he now considers 'terrible'. He even once appeared briefly on Grampian television show *A Touch of Music* playing the French horn, which they taped and which his father used to embarrass him with whenever he had girlfriends round. Between each section of the Mozart piece he was playing he indecorously wiped his nose on his sleeve, because as a teenager he thought it looked cool. 'They had to keep cutting to the pianist,' he said gleefully.

Heavily into Billy Idol in the early eighties, and with spiky hair held in place with lashings of hair gel, Ewan would get his kicks battering away at the drums in Scarlet Pride. Following the lead of seventies Scots pop sensations the Bay City Rollers and some of the New Romantic groups of the early eighties, Ewan wore black and white striped jeans with red bandannas around his knees and red paint in his hair for the few public appearances Scarlet Pride made.

He had other, more academic ambitions, despite being an unexceptional scholar at Morrison's Academy, the school he began attending in 1983. He was keen on writing, at which he was good at generating ideas, but not so good on basic practicalities like spelling and grammar. 'I've never been a good student,' he admitted candidly, 'and that was a bit of a sore spot for my parents because they're both teachers. I had a great love of music and art, but they don't really let you do that at school. They think you're copping off, which was a shame. When you get to the age where you choose your exam subjects, I wanted to do art and music. They said "No, that's not very serious, is it? You've got to do maths and chemistry." I said I was deadly serious. As a result, I became less and less interested in school.'

Whether he liked it or not, school played a very big part in the McGregors' family life. While Jim was a teacher, there were also deeper family connections with Morrison's Academy. Ewan McGregor's great-great-grandfather James had been a local stone mason in Crieff and had helped build the private school in 1860. His grandfather James McGregor had been a pupil, too. Carol (who was the daughter of a local jeweller Laurie and his shopkeeper wife Phyllis) and Jim had started going out with each other when they met as pupils at the school. They had married in July 1966, before moving to work in Glasgow, where their first son Colin was born in February 1969. When they returned to Crieff in 1970 Jim became the physical education teacher at the school and helped out with career advice for pupils. Meanwhile Carol took up a post at Crieff High School, before being promoted to deputy head-teacher at Kingspark School in Dundee.

The McGregors were essentially a very solid middle-class family, grounded in the community and open to education and new influences. This community involvement led Jim and Carol to establish the Crieff Film Society, often the only place locals could see recent movies as the local cinema had closed down. Undoubtedly an influence on their young son, this early exposure to cinema, along with films screened on TV, may help explain his overwhelming interest in film acting rather than the more traditional British route of performing on stage.

During his time at school, Ewan played the leading part in a production of a Moliere farce which required him to dress up in satin trousers and don a long wavy wig and a ZZ-Top style stick-on beard. One of the teachers involved in the production, Hector McMillan, noted that Ewan took his acting very seriously, discussing the role with the director, questioning motivation and creating his performance from those discussions. In 1983 he also appeared in the school production of Constance Cox's *The Caliph's Minstrel*.

Music, too, continued to play a part in Ewan's life at school and he won a prize for playing the French horn. However, despite his dramatic and musical successes, and reasonable academic results, Ewan felt that he lived in the shadow of his older brother Colin, who was a brilliant sportsman and scholar. Colin was the captain of the school and went on to become an RAF Tornado pilot. In comparison, Ewan felt his was a life more ordinary.

Like all teenagers, he desperately wanted to be popular at school, and set out to achieve that by joining every sub-culture going. 'I'd want to be a part of them all, instead of just being a member of one,' he admitted. 'It was a deep insecurity and an incredible desire to be loved and wanted, which is also a lot to do with acting: "Please like me! Everybody like me!" ' It also came from a deep seated jealousy of his brother's achievements which was a driving force behind his acting and workaholic nature.

Ewan found himself becoming the class clown, as many actors and comics have been, and he had frequent run-ins with his teachers over his lack of application to his academic work. Despite his parents being in the teaching profession, it was clear to staff at the Academy that Ewan didn't

'I have always been and I still am driven. I never let myself entertain the notion of what would happen if it didn't all work out.'

like his teachers and had problems with authority figures in general. The big problem was that the teachers Ewan crossed had easy access to his father to make a complaint. On one occasion, during a cross-country run, Ewan and his pal Malcolm Copland decide to skip even his Dad's class and opted for a detour via Ewan's nearby house. There he was found by his father – who'd apparently had the same idea – and was promptly punished by being made to pick up the litter scattered around the school grounds.

'It's not an easy thing to be told by your son, "I'm going to be an actor." I don't think it was an easy thing for them to hear, but they were always right behind me.'

His parents' openness in allowing Ewan to have access to religion in order that he make up his own mind had sparked a great deal of curiosity about the spiritual world. Aged fourteen he went on a Christian Outward Bound course, camping out under the stars, where he saw a shooting star, and he became even more interested in religion, to the extent of regularly attending Christian group meetings in Crieff.

Ewan now puts this down to a teenage phase, and blames puberty for his brief fling with organised religion. 'I look back on it with slight disgust,' he has said. 'Puberty is a confusing time, and they [religious groups] sink their talons into young flesh and they got me.' For eight long months Ewan was to be found preaching the Gospel to the bad kids at school, and went to church every Sunday, this time not simply for the chance to act in the parish play.

The spell was broken when he attended a Youth Fellowship evening about the evils of sex – a subject he was just beginning to get interested in – and how it was immoral before marriage. The Christian delivering the lecture was, Ewan knew from other kids at school, a man who happily beat his son. 'I just saw right through it,' he said, losing his religion right there and then.

Also aged fourteen, Ewan had a flirtation with the very Scottish world of golf, although he didn't play very well. 'In Scotland there's not the same elitist thing with golf,' he noted. 'We used to play on public courses, just for something to do. When I was fourteen I got thrown off a golf course for swearing. After every shot I would get really angry, screaming "Fuck!" Eventually this guy drove up in a tractor and told me I had to leave because the other golfers had been complaining. So, I had to walk back in shame with my clubs. I didn't play for a long while after that. I just got fed up being crap.'

That important factor in Ewan's abandonment of organised religion was a subject which pre-occupied him like all the other fourteen year-olds at Morrison's Academy. Within two years he had lost his virginity. He claims to have been taken in hand by an older girl, eager to provide his sexual enlightenment. 'Somebody took hold of me and gave me a good one. They were not that much older, but they seemed to have a good idea [of what they were doing]. It was great, I felt pretty good about it.'

At the age of sixteen, in 1987, Ewan was going out with Vicky McNally, now a married bank clerk in Crieff with the name Vicky Grant. Ewan's mother recalled girls being interested in her son since he'd been at primary school. He went out with McNally, on and off, for close to two years. The pair would often try to sneak into the empty private cinema below the ballroom at the Crieff Hydro, before being caught and thrown out by the porter.

An endemic problem in Scotland is that of under-age drinking, and the small town of Crieff is no exception. Ewan McGregor, Vicky McNally and Malcolm Copland were all part of a group of Crieff teenagers who would go to a small hotel, where they would get an illicit drink and smoke out of sight of their parents. In fact, McNally and Ewan would end their relationship with an argument over smoking. Ewan didn't like it when she started the habit he had already picked up, and despite claims made to his pals that he would give up the weed on his eighteenth birthday, he hasn't to this day. His liking for alcohol and tobacco – and his inability to stop – were signs of the potentially addictive personality he was later to develop.

Ewan McGregor claims to have known he would be an actor from the age of nine. Not only had he enjoyed watching his uncle in *Star Wars,* he had always had a love of classic black and white Hollywood movies and often watched them on weekend TV matinees. 'Saturday and Sunday, there'd be old black-and-white movies back-to-back on TV. Old romances from Hollywood and the British Ealing films from the forties and fifties.'

These films and the style of acting displayed in them made a huge impression on the young would-be actor. 'I loved how the blokes would underplay and the ladies were very theatrical,' he noted. 'If it was black-and-white and romantic and soppy, it was good enough for me. I didn't know what acting meant. I didn't know it meant you pretended to be another person. I suppose I thought about it in terms of being like one of the people in those films. But from then on, for me everything was geared towards finding out about it.'

Of all the films he'd seen, he loved *The Philadelphia Story* best and considered James Stewart his favourite actor of all time: 'You can't put your finger on it, really. He's just a beautiful actor.'

There were other influences too. Although he was never really to try and get into it himself, Ewan was fascinated by the conventions of Christmas pantomimes. 'Remember the principal boy was always played by a woman? It all became about legs and I fell in love with the leading ladies. So, it had a lot to do with sex.'

From the age of fourteen, Ewan was in regular contact with Perth Repertory Theatre, trying to get them to 'let me in to do something', not because he thought it was a prestigious theatre, but because it was the nearest to his home town of Crieff. To do so, though, would mean leaving school early and taking a huge risk.

Great pressure had been put on Ewan by his teacher parents to do well at school, although it was clear that academically he was never going to match the achievements of his older brother, Colin. Ewan reacted badly to the pressure, claiming that he was never going to need to understand subjects like maths. As an actor, he would have no need of such things. In the public exams, he managed to pass four O Grades – a merely average result – and couldn't face the prospect of returning for a fifth year at high school to sit his higher exams.

Neverthless, he was somewhat taken aback when his parents suddenly gave in, during the beginning of his fifth year at secondary school when he had started work for the Higher exams. 'I had become quite depressed – so I've been told – and started getting into trouble all the time,' claimed Ewan. 'And my mum said one day, "If you're unhappy, it's not necessarily going to do you much good to stay on." She was right, and it was a really brave decision for them to make.'

He had been having a difficult relationship with one teacher in particular, one who'd been encouraging in the past. 'She was a Jean Brodie type,' he said. 'We'd been quite close, but then she started pushing me in a particular direction. Anyway, I started answering back and she kept sending me to the headmaster . . . the whole thing became embarrassing.'

Jim and Carol knew from watching Denis struggle through years of hardship what a risk taking up a career as an actor would be, but they felt it was more important to let their son make his own mistakes and learn his own lessons than to force him to stay on at school to gain qualifications. It was particularly embarrassing for his father, as he was the school's careers adviser at the time.

'It's not an easy thing to be told by your son, "I'm going to be an actor." I don't think it was an easy thing for them to hear, but they were always right behind me,' said Ewan of his parents' support of his own ambitions. 'They put me through drama school and sold things so that I could go.'

As soon as the decision was taken, Ewan decided to finish with school immediately and set off on his theatrical adventure. 'I came back to school and went into the fifth year, when my brother had been Head Boy in 1987/88. I did maybe five or six weeks and then I bailed out. I don't regret it at all,' he told pupils of Morrison's Academy during a return visit to the school in 1997. 'What I do regret, however, is not having realised that what you are taught in school is maybe valid. I never really made the connection that what you were being taught was useful in any way. I never thought it was and I was wrong in that respect. I left and I started working straight away in the theatre, which was what I wanted to do.'

CHAPTER 2

JEDI IN TRAINING

ONLY THREE DAYS AFTER LEAVING MORRISON'S ACADEMY, aged just sixteen, in October 1987 Ewan McGregor managed to secure himself a job as a stagehand at Perth Theatre. It meant travelling between Crieff and Perth in a battered old green Volkswagen Beetle, but it was the first rung on the acting ladder for McGregor.

His decision to go to Perth meant leaving behind his friends. One school pal in particular – Malcolm Copland, who'd been a sympathetic figure throughout McGregor's sixteen years in Crieff – told the young would-be actor to his face that he was making a mistake and throwing away his life. McGregor was sorry that his decision was to lead to the end of the friendship, but having finally persuaded his parents to back his desire to choose his own path, he wasn't about to let a school friend deflect him, either.

It was the intervention of his mother that had persuaded Joan Knight, then director of the Perth Theatre, to hire Ewan at the princely sum of £50 a week as a general stagehand. Of course, Ewan was far more interested in the recently established Perth Youth Theatre Group. For Liz Carruthers, director of the Youth Theatre Group workshops, the sixteen year-old didn't particularly stand out from the crowd. But while his acting didn't impress, it was noticed that he was taking a deep interest in all aspects of stage craft, from acting to working the spotlights and discovering exactly what a 'director' actually did.

As an all-rounder at Perth Theatre, where he pulled the curtains, made the tea and worked on the costumes, Ewan found himself learning invaluable lessons. These lessons were as much social as professional. He found himself mixing with people much older than he was, people who had already made careers out of stage work, whether behind the scenes or in front of the spotlights. He found himself drifting away from life and friends in Crieff, including his girlfriend Vicky McNally, but it was a period of much-needed growth for a young man in a hurry.

'There's a point, about two weeks before you shoot, where you think, maybe this is the role I won't be able to crack, but the pace keeps you well-oiled.'

He also made his professional acting debut with the group, in October 1987 when he was an extra in an adaptation of E. M. Forster's *A Passage to India*. He is credited in the programme under 'Servants and others'. 'I was running about with a turban and all blacked up.'

It may have been an inauspicious start for the future star of *Trainspotting*, but his six months at Perth Repertory Theatre gave Ewan a solid grounding in the basics of the theatrical world. Early in 1988 he would make an uncredited appearance in the play *Pravda*. Naturally, his youthful enthusiasm sometimes overwhelmed him, something he was happy to concede many years later. 'I was an arsehole, being far too keen,' he admitted of his time at Perth, 'trying to make everyone like me, trying to learn about everything at once.'

A major task for him at Perth was to move the scenery on stage, sometimes during performances when he'd have to do it in costume to fit in with the play being performed. It was minor stuff, but it was a chance for him to appear on stage regularly before a paying audience – even if he had no dialogue to deliver. 'I'd always be there [on stage] just slightly longer than anybody else, you know, just to get my stage time in,' he said of his first attempts to hog the limelight.

Following his time at Perth, Ewan enrolled for a one-year foundation course in drama at Kirkcaldy College of Technology. Places were very much sought after, as the course only took 26 people each year.

Ewan had to go through an interview and an audition process, before joining in with a variety of 'dramatic exercises' with other hopeful applicants. It was here that his time at Perth came in useful. This was way above playing in the church panto or messing about in school productions. This was the first step on a serious acting career – and he had to come across as a serious-minded professional who also had the talent required to go far.

At the age of seventeen, in August 1988, Ewan left home. The travelling back and forwards between Crieff and Perth for his six-month stint at the theatre there had been gruelling but worthwhile. Now he had to stand on his own two feet and decided to move into halls of residence in Kirkcaldy, as the town was even further away, across the Firth of Forth from Edinburgh. It was a big step for a young lad who'd always had the support and sympathy of his parents and his brother to fall back on.

Kirkcaldy College was mainly a technical college, offering practical courses, and the Higher National Certificate Theatre Arts Programme seemed to sit a little uneasily with the other courses available. The course consisted of a series of discrete modules which were supposed to result in four complete drama productions each year. In the first term, McGregor found himself drawing on the more technical stage skills he'd learnt at Perth as he stage managed a group revue. He didn't begin to compete immediately for leading acting roles, preferring to lurk behind the scenes until he got the lie of the land.

One notable part that he did play was in a second term student performance of *The Prime of Miss Jean Brodie*. Ewan tackled the role of the staid music teacher Mr Lowther who marries Brodie, which he and his tutors saw as a much more demanding character than the perhaps more obviously attractive role of Brodie's lover. Taking to the stage in earnest struck a deep chord. 'I realised this was exactly what I wanted to do, that I hadn't been mistaken all this time.'

The third term saw him take a leading part in a comedy parody of Arthur Miller's *A View from a Bridge*, punningly retitled *A Few from the Fridge*, in which he also had stage management duties. This production even went on the road, with performances mounted in theatre workshops in both Glasgow and Edinburgh. It was a large amount of responsibility for a mere seventeen-year-old, but McGregor lapped up the opportunity to put his skills to a practical use. He began to feel that he was only really alive when he was performing or working on a production.

During the time at college, Ewan did not have much of a social life beyond the occasional pint in the local pubs and the odd night at Jackie O's night-club in the town. However, away from the restrictions of home, he was ready to take advantage of any opportunities that came along and during the nine months of the course, he had four relationships – three fleeting and one far more serious. The serious one started when he met Hannah Titley. She was the same age as him, had come from London and was looking to develop a career in stage management rather than as an actress. She and McGregor developed a deep and lasting relationship. The pair hung out together in Kirkcaldy, enjoying the limited night life and pouring their efforts into their studies

The Kirkcaldy course finished in summer 1989 and the prospect of auditioning for drama school in London loomed. It was the natural next move for any ambitious young actor. Perth and Kirkcaldy had been all very well, but deep down, Ewan knew that at some point he would have to relocate to London to build a lasting career. But there was also Hannah to consider. They were serious about each other, and he agreed to move in with her to a flat in Edinburgh.

Hannah had secured a place across the Forth Bridge on a Stage Management Course at the city's Queen Margaret College. The world-famous Fringe Festival must have been a tempting proposition for the thespian ambitions of these ex-students from Kirkcaldy College of Technology, but Ewan was determined to be different. Rather than step out on a public stage while he was still learning his craft, he worked as a waiter at Gennaro's Italian Restaurant in Edinburgh's Grassmarket. Waiter Paolo Diotaiuti remembers that the aspiring actor would often get good tips, especially from women diners. He was a confident young man who would put on a little performance as he worked the tables, especially tables filled with attractive young women.

It was tempting for the young actor to think the summer of 1989 would never end. He was living with his girlfriend in a wonderful city, and although not acting, he was working and earning a little money. The pair had discussed their relationship and McGregor's acting ambitions and how the two might co-exist. They agreed the relationship must come first, but in his heart Ewan knew that he was also preparing to take the final step to achieve the ambition he'd harboured since the age of nine.

Just as there was only one place to go to pursue his acting ambitions, there was one place in London that had to be his first port of call – the prestigious Royal Academy of Dramatic Arts (RADA).

'I came down to London to audition for drama schools,' Ewan later told veteran TV interviewer Michael Parkinson. 'My first one was at RADA. They charged you £30 or something, and I didn't have any money. It was £60 for the train fare, so I came down and had spent the better part of £100. I walked into a room and there was one guy behind a desk to tell people whether they should become actors or not – you'd have thought they'd have two or three. I can't remember his name. I walked in, I was seventeen and determined to get in. He didn't want to hear any speeches, but just wanted to have a chat. He asked my age. I said I was seventeen and he said, "You have a good few years of auditioning ahead of you".'

The rejection by RADA was the first setback Ewan had suffered. 'I said to him, "Excuse me? I've just spent the better part of £100 and you've written me off already?" That was RADA. I just hope that they're sorry now!' Recovering from the shock, he worked up the courage to begin applying elsewhere, and he was quickly granted an interview at the Guildhall School of Music and Drama in London. He had half a day to impress his would-be tutors. He managed it, with a combination of improvisation, prepared speeches and even a song, sung on request, and was invited back for a more formal two-day auditioning process.

Despite his experience, natural confidence and self-belief, Ewan claims he felt self-conscious among so many other would-be actors. His experiences dented his confidence as an actor, which was more a result of being away from friends and family, from the familiar and comfortable in Scotland, for the first time. 'I didn't want to be – and I don't want this to sound the wrong way – a "Scottish" actor,' said Ewan of his arrival in London. 'I'm the most fiercely proud Scotsman you'll ever meet, and I love Scotland, and it's a huge important thing in my life that I'm Scottish, but I wanted to be able to do everything.'

At the audition, he was asked to pretend to be a piece of elastic. 'I'm not a cerebral actor, so I didn't think, "How can I portray elastic?" I just tried to become a piece of elastic. I was doing alright – I thought, "yeah, I'm pretty fucking elastic, baby!"' Then he was told by the person conducting the audition not to use his arms. 'I almost said "Don't be fucking ridiculous – how can I be elastic without using my arms?"' Of the 700 applicants and the 100 in the second stage, he was just one of 24 students selected for the three-year course, where he was to be taught mime and traditional drama by Kenneth Rea.

He was now eighteen and felt he'd left some of his more childish attempts at acting back in Scotland – the playground versions of Princess Leia, Olivia Newton-John and Elvis Presley – but here he was getting into the Guildhall College in London 'by pretending to be an elastic band'!

What being at college taught him most was 'getting used to living in London. I always thought I was fantastic until I got to drama school, where that notion was soundly thrashed out. I don't know whether college can teach you to be a great actor.'

Ewan's self-confidence was further damaged at a meet-and-greet session early on in the course where all the students were asked to share their life stories. One after another, his contemporaries poured out heartfelt tales of tragedy and struggle. As it came closer and closer to Ewan's turn, he began to panic as his childhood held no such tales. 'I didn't seem to have any, I was going "Fuck it. I'm never going to make it. I'm obviously not of the right stock – I didn't suffer enough." Now it just annoys me. Actors feel that they have to suffer; that everything has to come from a point of pain.' It's a view of acting which Ewan doesn't agree with, refusing to succumb to the ever-fashionable Method.

While at the Guildhall, McGregor began writing songs again, for the first time since his teenage days with Scarlet Pride. He showed signs that he hadn't given up entirely on his pop ambitions, or that he was preparing in case he failed his drama course and wanted to explore music as a possible alternative. To that end he used to go busking with an actor friend, Zubin Varla, staking out a spot in Bank tube station in the City. 'We made about £20 an hour,' he remembered, wryly. Calling themselves Mano Et Mano, he and Varla also played in a vegetarian restaurant in Clapham.

'I came down to London to audition for drama schools. My first one was at RADA. He asked my age. I said I was seventeen and he said, "You have a good few years of auditioning ahead of you" . . . That was RADA. I just hope that they're sorry now!'

Ewan had started life in London as a long-term resident at the YMCA near the Guildhall in the city's financial district at the height of the 'yuppie boom' of the late eighties. He felt out-of-place and even out of his depth in London, which was somewhat overwhelming when compared to Crieff, Perth and Kirkcaldy. Even Edinburgh, for all its cosmopolitan attractions, could not compete for sheer scale and numbers of people.

The Guildhall, in the Barbican complex – not one of London's more attractive architectural achievements – was a very different institution from Kirkcaldy College. A much more rigorous and professional course was in place, lasting three years and aiming to prepare the students to become the major actors of the future. The first year provided a basic grounding in technique, something Ewan found relatively easy as he seemed to have been displaying a natural ability all his life. Only in the second year would performances be staged – and this would include a tour around Europe, where Ewan featured in numerous nightly performances of Shakespeare's *As You Like It* in places as diverse as Istanbul and Hamburg.

The biggest pressure he felt during the first year was in keeping his relationship going with Hannah. Although they spoke often on the phone and would sometimes visit each other, it was plain towards the end of his first year on the course that they were drifting further and further apart. They had different groups of friends, different social experiences and different environments. They simply couldn't keep the same level of intimacy that they had enjoyed now that they were 400 miles apart most of the time. Deep down Ewan had understood this the day he had first stepped on the train at Waverley station in Edinburgh to move down to London. After a heart-to-heart, they decided to go their separate ways. Nevertheless, they remained close friends and managed to still see each other regularly.

After splitting with Hannah, Ewan moved out of the YMCA and lived successively in a couple of run-down flats on the notorious Kingsmead Estate in Hackney. Despite the reputation of the area for being a crime blackspot, he claimed never to have seen anything untoward, and he lived in another flat in Hackney before finally settling in a shared student flat in Leytonstone.

By the time he was entering his third year at the Guildhall, Ewan realised what he'd gained from the tough processes he'd undergone. He'd arrived thinking he knew all he had to know about acting from his previous courses and minimal practical experience, but the Guildhall course had shown him that there was more to the profession than he'd ever imagined lying in front of the TV as a teenager absorbing the performances of Cary Grant and James Stewart. He'd just begun to think of the next step in the process – finding an agent and securing auditions for any television or film bit parts he could find – when fate came knocking on his door.

Just before leaving his acting course at Guildhall in March 1992 Ewan had been spotted by actor's agent Lindy King of Jonathan Altaras Associates. This was in January 1992 at the Guildhall's open evening, when over 100 of London's theatrical talent agents and directors gathered to check out the latest crop of forthcoming drama graduates in an evening of individual and ensemble performances.

'It was the scariest fucking thing in the world,' recalled Ewan of his turn during the open evening. He bravely tackled a Barbara Streisand musical number 'Gettin' It Together, Step by Step'. 'A terrible fucking number,' he remembered. His set was wrapped up with 'Lean on Me', with the middle section filled out with some dialogue from the Bruce Robinson film *Withnail and I* (a student favourite), and a monologue he'd written himself – with a hefty dose of assistance from Denis Lawson – about an oil worker who'd lost his legs in a terrible accident on an oil rig.

McGregor used a wheelchair for this self-penned role, wheeling himself out onto an empty stage. Halfway through delivering his speech the young actor froze, the next section of his monologue vanishing from his mind. All he could think to do was look down and play with the fake leg stump he'd attached in order to add to the realism of the performance. He then slowly wheeled himself off stage, thinking his acting career was well and truly over before it had begun.

'I came off and I thought: "Fuck, that's it, I've blown it,"' Ewan recalled. 'And then I found out that I hadn't, much to my surprise.'

Getting an agent was only the beginning, but things moved incredibly quickly. Ewan was sent off to audition for the leading role of Private Mick Hopper in *Lipstick on Your Collar*, a six-part television series written by Dennis Potter. Knowing who Potter was, Ewan didn't think he had much chance of winning a leading part like this first time out. However, luckily for him, television producer Rosemarie Whitman had all but given up hope of finding the right actor for the lead role. She needed someone who could not only act, but sing and dance too. The part would require considerable amounts of lip-synching, matching mimed singing to backing tracks, and it was proving to be a talent that was in short supply.

Although aware that she was taking a risk with an unproven talent straight out of drama school in a highly visible leading role, Whitman felt she had little choice. This young, fresh-faced enthusiastic actor was just perfect for the difficult-to-fill part. For Ewan, all those theatrical turns performed at his parents' parties in the seventies, where he perfected his Elvis Presley impersonations, were about to pay off.

To his surprise, Ewan was signed up for the six-episode series and quickly negotiated to leave the Guildhall earlier than he otherwise would have. After all, he argued, wasn't the point of the course to train actors to be able to win parts? He'd done that, so didn't want to miss out on what seemed more and more like a potential big break simply because his course had a few months to go. The authorities at the Guildhall agreed, and released him.

Dennis Potter was an active and often controversial force in British television drama for 30 years. He'd come to prominence in the sixties with contributions to the then-popular genre of one-off television plays, where his works included *Alice* and *Vote, Vote, Vote for Nigel Barton* and *Stand Up for Nigel Barton.* He then built on his growing reputation in the seventies where he was especially prolific, writing a six part dramatised biography of Casanova, a seven part adaptation of Thomas Hardy's *The Mayor of Casterbridge* and the classic *Pennies from Heaven.*

Potter was at this time also writing for the BBC's *Play for Today* series, including 1979's *Blue Remembered Hills*, which had a group of seven-year-old children playing and fighting in the country on a day in 1943, all played by adult actors. More controversial was 1976's *Brimstone and Treacle*, which was about the demonic seduction of a handicapped child. It was pulled from the schedules and not shown until 1987, some eleven years after being made.

In the eighties, Potter consolidated his reputation with a trio of plays from his own production company, *Blade on the Feather*, *Rain on the Roof* and *Cream in My Coffee*, all broadcast in 1980 . He would return to the BBC, in the mid eighties, culminating in his award winning six-part noir medical thriller *The Singing Detective*, starring Michael Gambon. The late eighties and early nineties saw Potter gain more control over his television productions, but he also seemed to lose his magic touch, battling his own diseases, demons and illness. In 1988 he adapted the coolly received *Christabel* from Christabel Bielenberg's memoirs of life in Nazi Germany, *The Past is Myself*, starring Elizabeth Hurley and then *Blackeyes* which he both wrote and directed. Finally, cancer of the pancreas killed him on 17 June 1994, after a very public battle to finish his last two works, *Karaoke* and *Cold Lazarus.*

Lipstick on Your Collar in 1993 would go some way to restoring Potter's by - then tarnished critical and public reputation. He saw the project as the final part of his musical trilogy, with *Pennies from Heaven* dealing with the thirties, *The Singing Detective* covering the forties and *Lipstick on Your Collar* tackling the fifties, with appropriate musical styles.

In this comedy-drama, a young private, Mick Hopper (McGregor), doing his National Service in the Army, falls in love with his voluptuous neighbour (Louise Germaine) who happens to be married to his superior. He spends his days translating meaningless Russian memos as a means of regulating the Cold War. His real passion, though, is for the band with whom he plays in the evenings and at weekends.

The series featured rock'n'roll, and, in classic Potter fantasy style, used song and dance numbers to advance the story and relate the interior thoughts and feelings of his characters. Full of enthusiasm and self-confidence, Ewan threw himself into the role with abandon. Shooting began in March 1992, just before he celebrated his 21st birthday – an event which brought production to a halt as a surprise birthday cake was presented to him in the studio. The series was shot at Twickenham Studios in London, Pinewood Studios in Buckinghamshire and on locations throughout London. Hair died black and complexion cleaned up with a series of facials, Ewan was ready to face the world as the star of a major television production.

. . . and I love Scotland, and it's a huge important thing in my life I'm Scottish.'

'You always think you'll never work again. But on the scale of things in this business, I've been the luckiest man alive.'

Plucked straight from drama school, Ewan tackled his first professional role as Mick Hopper in Dennis Potter's Lipstick on Your Collar.

Ewan McGregor was not at all bothered by the approaching controversy – he was more concerned with learning all he could about how movies and television were made - and he knew Dennis Potter was the man to talk to. 'He'd talk to me and warn me about what might happen after this came out, and about my responsibility to my talent.'

After production was completed, Ewan found himself frustrated and at a loose end. 'I was

'Dennis Potter would talk to me and warn me about what might happen after Lipstick came out, and about my responsibility to my talent.'

waiting for six months for it to come out, looking at the date in my calendar,' he remembered of the tense time between completing the shooting of the six episodes and their broadcast on Channel 4. 'I really, truly believed that the day after the first episode came out my life would be changed.'

Ewan's life wasn't changed overnight, of course. When the phone didn't ring and nothing dramatic happened, he found himself returning to reality. To him *Lipstick on Your Collar* was a big break and the first step toward a career, to viewers it was just another programme, if a mildly controversial one. 'It's telly,' said McGregor, years later. 'It's there for an hour, then it's gone.'

Immediately afterwards, he was out of work for four months. Most other actors would regard such a rest as minor, but for workaholic McGregor the hiatus between roles was almost unbearable. He began to fear that *Lipstick on Your Collar* would be his only acting experience. He wanted to be a working actor, a jobbing actor, who went from role to role, part to part almost continuously.

The memory of this period of unemployment would drive Ewan to commit to film after film as his career took off. He always found it hard to say no to a part as, despite his huge self-confidence, he was haunted by an almost contradictory and constant fear that the work would dry up and he'd never step out before a camera again. It was an insecurity that he has never really overcome, no matter how successful he has been.

Moreover, he wasn't entirely idle between *Lipstick on Your Collar* and his next major role. He resorted to that trusty stand-by of many rising British actors, the voice-over for adverts, doing a series of TV spots for St Ivel Gold butter, among others. McGregor also appeared in a couple of radio productions broadcast on the BBC World Service in 1992. In Spanish playwright Alfonso Sastre's meditation on political terrorism, *Tragic Prelude*, McGregor played Oscar, a disillusioned political activist who accidentally kills his own brother. In Tom Stoppard's *The Real Thing*, McGregor won the small but pivotal role of a soldier-playwright, with Emily Woof, whom he would meet again when making *Velvet Goldmine*.

He worked the rounds of television auditions very hard, among them one for the part of Julien Sorel in an adaptation of Stendal's classic novel, *Scarlet and Black*. His agent was called afterwards and the call was brief: Ewan was not what they were looking for. It was a story he was familiar with, but this time he wasn't going to take it lying down.

The producers of *Scarlet and Black* wanted a raven-haired, jutting-jawed romantic hero capable of swashbuckling, shooting and seducing his way through nineteenth-century Paris. Weedy (he is a thin 5ft' 10in.), Scottish and blondish, Ewan McGregor just wasn't it. Director Ben Bolt and producer Ros Wolfes were considering Ewan's pal Jude Law for the role instead.

Ewan went back in fighting. 'I knew I simply had to go back there and prove to them that I was what they were looking for. The result was that they dyed my hair.' It was another triumph for the now famous McGregor self-belief, and Jude Law would have to wait for movies like *Wilde* and *Gattaca* for his big break. (He wouldn't hold this role-pinching against McGregor, though, joining him in 1995 to set up the production company Natural Nylon.)

First published in 1830, Stendahl's novel – subtitled *A Chronicle of the Nineteenth Century* – was read by the contemporary French public against the background of an ideological struggle between liberals, holding republican views, and ultra-royalists, who fervently supported Charles X. The story after the determined rise of Julian Sorel, after his decision that the route to power was no longer through the army (the scarlet of the title) but through the Church (the black).

Ben Bolt directed the three-part adaptation for the BBC, with a cast including Martin Jarvis, Alice Krige, T. P. McKenna, Stratford Johns and Rachel Weisz.

As soon as he'd won the role, having persuaded the BBC producers that he was the only man

As Julien Sorel, the swashbuckling, romantic hero in Scarlet & Black.

'I was scared. But the final straw was when a fellow actor told me that, bar Hamlet, this has to be the best part for a young actor.'

for the job, Ewan's confidence collapsed in a sudden bout of self-doubt. It was the negative partner of his self-belief striking back. What if *Lipstick on Your Collar* had been a lucky chance of being the right person for the part? This was a very different type of production – a wordy yet action-packed costume drama. He didn't have a great deal of experience – what if he wasn't up to it after all? Just one week before rehearsals were due to begin, Ewan thought seriously about pulling out altogether. If he had, it would likely have meant the end of his acting career.

'I had a complete crisis,' he later admitted. 'I suddenly felt crushed by the weight of the responsibility inherent in the part - and genuinely doubted that I was up to it. I was scared. But the final straw was when a fellow actor told me that, bar Hamlet, this has to be the best part for a young actor.'

A trip back to Scotland and the family home in Crieff helped to restore his confidence, and a few weeks later he was on a plane to France to begin filming on the series. It was to be the only moment when the young actor was almost overwhelmed by a fear of success.

One problem Ewan faced on *Scarlet and Black* was tackling its love scenes. In 1992 he'd shot a love scene for *Lipstick on Your Collar*, but as the girl was fully clothed and they were on a turntable, McGregor claimed it didn't count. 'Love scenes can be embarrassing and they can be really lovely too,' he has admitted. 'I'm quite open about it, in that I'm not embarrassed by nudity. I've been driven to work in the morning, taken my clothes off, been made up, spent all day in bed with somebody, pretending to make love.'

His bedroom work on *Scarlet and Black* was to be a taste of things to come, as in many of his later roles he wouldn't hesitate to lose his clothes on screen. 'Anyone who says you feel nothing because it's all technical is lying,' he said of shooting romantic scenes for the camera. 'In fact, the camera crew adds a certain frisson to proceedings.' He even persuaded the director Ben Bolt to let him streak through a French field for one scene.

When it was all over, Ewan was glad to escape the costume drama trappings. 'I remember somebody asked me what I was going to do after *Scarlet and Black*, and I said I didn't know. The only thing I hoped was that it would be something in jeans with a Scottish accent and no bloody cravat.'

Despite his desire to do other films, Ewan began to exhibit a tentative interest in other forms of expressing the actor's craft. 'I know I want to get back and do some theatre and I wouldn't mind giving Hollywood a go if the role was right, but that's it,' he said of his career plans at the time. Unlike his contemporary, actor John Hannah – best known for *Four Weddings and a Funeral* and *Sliding Doors,* and his co-star in the radio drama *The Real Thing* – Ewan had not taken the opportunities available in Britain for actors to play roles in live theatre. But in the New Year of 1993 he took on a part in Joe Orton's *What the Butler Saw.*

Panned upon its debut in 1969, Orton's play had gone on to be regarded as a modern classic. Ewan featured as page boy Nick in a production by Penny Cineiwicz mounted at the Salisbury Playhouse. While he enjoyed the production – especially shocking the good citizens of Salisbury when he had to disrobe on stage – Ewan didn't feel the spark in theatre that'd he'd got when performing in front of the television cameras.

It was tiresome playing the same material night after night, compared to the swift run-through of feature film or television serial production. He found himself bored on stage – and that led to the temptation to start acting up. He decided that he definitely preferred acting for the screen to the stage. It was a decision he wouldn't reconsider until the autumn of 1998.

Since splitting up with Hannah Titley, Ewan had not had a serious relationship. There'd been girlfriends, of course, but nothing had developed beyond a few weeks' fun and companionship. He wasn't looking for anything more, so he was surprised when he found himself falling for French woman Marie Pairis while shooting *Scarlet and Black* on location.

Pairis was the 'crowd wrangler', in charge of marshalling the extras for the historical scenes. The pair struck up a friendship almost immediately, and their relationship quickly became physical, while the rest of the cast and crew of the production remained almost totally oblivious.

Pairis was short and brunette, and became the subject of speculation when Ewan mentioned his current girlfriend in interviews to promote *Scarlet and Black*, although he refused to elaborate. 'I am besotted with a beautiful Frenchwoman,' he confided. 'It is providing me with huge bouts of joy and happiness.' It was a *grande passion* – one he was determined to keep to himself as much as possible.

He and Pairis celebrated the end of shooting on *Scarlet and Black* with a motorbike tour of the Alps, with Ewan scaling the heights clinging to Pairis on the back of her BMW bike. This trip was to give McGregor an enduring interest in bikes, leading him to purchase a couple of his own. After the trip they had a decision to make, as he was returning to London to continue developing his acting career. She decided to join him and hoped to find some work once she got there. Ewan declared himself delighted with this turn of events, but – as with his relationship with Hannah Titley – he harboured doubts even before the relationship had gone very far. Denying any desire for marriage or children, he had the feeling that Marie wasn't going to be the big love of his life.

Ewan made his first appearance in a short film thanks to the Lloyd's Bank Film Challenge scheme, which aimed to give a kick start to young film-making talents, especially writers and directors. *Family Style*, an eleven-minute black and white short, was one of the first projects to benefit from the scheme. Young writer Matthew Cooper from Leeds was seventeen and unemployed in 1993 when his screenplay was selected for development. His script was handed to 24-year-old director Justin Chadwick, a Leicester Polytechnic graduate, who had the task of casting and making the movie. It was eventually broadcast on Channel 4.

Family Style set out to capture the emotions that arise from a bereavement on a north-country farm. It opens in a cemetery, with nineteen-year-old Jimmie (Ewan) watching as the coffin containing the body of his older brother Stevie is lowered into a grave. Stevie, who is idolised by Jimmie, was killed in a car crash and the wrecked remains of the vehicle lie dumped outside the front of the family's farmhouse, a monument to a life wasted.

Against this bleak backdrop, Jimmie is faced with deciding whether to follow in Stevie's footsteps and leave for the bright lights of the city. His pent-up anger and frustrations lead to a violent physical expression in a battle with his father, who is attempting to sell the land where he grew up. Blood is finally shed, but when Jimmie's girlfriend Julie (Amelia Curtis) reveals she's pregnant, the frustrated teenager begins to see some kind of hope for the future.

This was a minor project by most standards, but Ewan didn't approach it any differently from the multi-part serial of *Lipstick on Your Collar* or the big-budget costume drama of *Scarlet and Black*. The finished product turned out to be something the young actor was extremely proud of. 'I've never had a show reel as such,' admitted McGregor. 'I was so proud of that film that I showed it to a lot of people. It's been really useful to me.'

Even before *Scarlet and Black*, Ewan had already made his feature film debut – but it was a tiny part in a film which was barely released almost two years after it had been shot. 'I spent a month dossing in Morocco, to do one line,' was how he remembered his first genuine movie experience, on Bill Forsyth's ill-fated Robin Williams vehicle, *Being Human*. 'It was fantastic – "I'll do it, Don Paolo" I said in a thick Glaswegian accent. I can remember the night before asking another actor, "Are you going to do it in Scots?" Stupid, the night before I had my big day.'

McGregor played the minor role of a volunteer hangman after a shipwreck. 'I was a Portuguese sailor called Alvarez, but I did it in a thick Glaswegian accent – and they cut "Don Paolo"!'

Despite the problems of the production and post-production of *Being Human*, Ewan had gained much from simply being on a movie set, even if he only made a fleeting appearance in the final cut. 'A movie set is a huge social occasion for me,' he said later. 'There's always wonderful, exciting people. You're learning all the time. But I've always found that the actors who try to teach you how to do it are always the ones you don't want to learn from. A lot of older guys do that. "Oh, sonny, here, this is how you do it." And I'm always saying, "Fuck off, that's not how I want to do it." The people you just observe are the ones you learn the most from. It should be about surprising everyone and yourself, doing a take and thinking, I didn't know that was going to happen!'

With two significant leading roles in major drama series under his belt, a couple of radio dramas, a short film and a very short appearance in a feature film, Ewan McGregor was spreading his acting wings.

He was ready for new challenges. Aged just 23 and clearly a star in the making, he claimed he always knew success – one way or another – would be his. 'I have always been and I still am driven. I don't know where to. I don't have any goal, or any goals, as such. This was always the way it was going to be and, in an arrogant fashion, I never let myself entertain the notion of what would happen if it didn't all work out.'

... inherent in the part, and genuinely doubted that I was up to it.'

CHAPTER 3
DIGGING DEEP

HIS TRAINING AT THE GUILDHALL and his television apprenticeship now all but over, what Ewan needed in 1993 was a movie role that would get him noticed. British cinema has gone through more ups and downs in the post-war period than the most extravagant roller-coaster, but it was in the low-budget world of most British films that he knew he'd have to start out if he was ever to stand a chance of working in Hollywood, the real home of commercial cinema.

The role he was waiting for turned out to be the starring part of Alex Law, the cocky, brash, arrogant – but charming – young Scottish journalist in a shocking, low - budget, high-concept, thriller, *Shallow Grave*. Long before he was cast, though, the film had endured a slow gestation.

Shallow Grave had begun with the meeting of two enthusiastic young Scots – Andrew Macdonald and John Hodge. Macdonald already had at least one foot in the door of the world of British film-making as his grandfather was Emeric Pressburger, partner of Michael Powell. Between them Powell and Pressburger produced a series of inspired films from the wartime satire *The Life and Death of Colonel Blimp* (1943), through the supernatural thrills of *A Matter of Life and Death* (1946), which proved an inspiration for Macdonald's own *A Life Less Ordinary*, to the fairy-tale beauty of *The Red Shoes* (1948).

Having left school in 1984, Macdonald helped out at the National Film and Television School, although he was not a student himself. He was soon working in the industry, albeit as a lowly 'runner' (a glorified messenger) on the Hugh Hudson flop *Revolution* (1985). He then spent a year working for a firm that made commercials. Keen to embark on a film-making career, he went to the United States to study producing at the American Film Institute, where he also gained employment as a script reader. That led to a minor production role on the Bridget Fonda vehicle *Shag* (1988). He returned to the UK and worked as an assistant director on *Venus Peter* (1989), location director on *The Big Man* (1990) and location manager on Terence Davies's *The Long Day Closes* (1992). Coming back to Scotland he worked on the Scottish Television series *The Advocates* and *Taggart*, before producing his own seven-part series called *Shadowing*. All this experience was to come in very handy when working on location and to very tight budgets on *Shallow Grave*.

Macdonald was making shorts when he met John Hodge at the Edinburgh International Film Festival in August 1991. One of Macdonald's shorts, *Dr Reitzer's Fragment*, was screening at the festival and Hodge's sister, Grace, had worked on it as a sound editor.

John Hodge was a junior doctor – both his parents had been GPs – with a burning desire to write a film script: 'I began writing *Shallow Grave* in the spring of 1991,' he said. 'I knew nothing and no-one. I naively assumed all I had to do was write what I like and all the necessary people would fall into place, take my script and turn it into the film I wanted to see.'

Hodge's idea for a movie was perfectly simple and simply perfect. 'I had this idea about three people in a flat and a stranger and a bag of money. That seemed to me like a film, so I began writing. The first draft of *Shallow Grave* was hand-written on napkins and the backs of envelopes.'

Hodge was introduced by Grace to Macdonald, who recognised the core of a brilliant idea. 'John had in his hand the proverbial foolscap hand-written notes,' Macdonald recalled of their meeting in a pub in Edinburgh in 1991. 'But already the basic story for *Shallow Grave* was there – the three flatmates, the interview scenes, the corpse and the money.'

From that meeting the pair embarked upon a semi-professional rewrite, hoping to get the ideas and story into a form which might attract interest from a film production company. 'Macdonald and I established a healthy working relationship,' remembered Hodge, who was still working as a doctor during the revision. 'I would write a new draft of the script which he would then read and then return with a tactful critique like, "The second half isn't up to much." Holding back the tears, I would review the section in question and, to my regular irritation, find myself in agreement. I then indulged in orgies of bloodletting, striking out sub-plots, characters and locations, and a couple of months later we would do it all over again.'

It was a tortuous process which took over a year and a half before the script was ready to be shown to possible financiers. With his producer's hat on Macdonald was aware that he had to keep the budget as low as possible, which meant persuading Hodge to limit his characters, limit his locations and limit the action the script demanded, while still telling a captivating, exciting and imaginative story. It was a tall order. 'With the script of *Shallow Grave* it was important that something happened every page or so. I didn't want it to be a study of character for its own sake; that character should be grafted onto a healthy narrative, rather than the narrative acting as an afterthought to give some expression of humanity. In this way, the story moves so quickly that there's no time for the characters to spend heart-searching over the rights and wrongs of their actions, they just go out and do it. I think this decisiveness and the way they enter into it with such enthusiasm will hook the audience as much as any moral questions.'

Finally, Hodge and Macdonald plucked up enough courage to send the screenplay off to the Scottish Film Production Fund with a request for development money. 'I didn't think they'd like it,' claimed Macdonald later. 'I thought it was the wrong type of story and the wrong type of film, given the projects they'd previously backed, so although I knew John's work was very good, I was actually quite surprised when they gave us the money. Allan Scott [screenwriter for many Nicolas Roeg movies and chairman of the SFPF] particularly liked it and rang us up to say that it was the best script, the best opening 30 pages, he'd read in years.'

In November 1992, while Ewan McGregor was finishing shooting Dennis Potter's *Lipstick on Your Collar*, Macdonald and Hodge were attending Movie Makers, a week long session held in Inverness by the Scottish Film Council in order to bring young would-be film-makers and screenwriters together with influential figures in the industry. It was here that Macdonald and Hodge met David Aukin, then Head of Drama at Channel 4, a British independent television station with a strong track record in supporting risky, low-budget British films. Aukin was very supportive of their project and invited them to a meeting at Channel 4.

The pair were instructed to come back with a fresh draft of the script, a budget proposal and a director attached. Early in 1993, just as *Lipstick on Your Collar* was being transmitted on Channel 4, *Shallow Grave* was given a green light and a production budget of £1 million, with £150,000 from the Glasgow Film Production Fund, a recent initiative designed to encourage the making of feature films in the city. *Shallow Grave* was to be the first film to benefit from the scheme, and the cost of local crews, construction teams and caterers was to mean that the city would see a return of four to five times the original investment, silencing critics who claimed that the fund was taking a huge risk putting so much money into one production.

With the finance in place, it was time for Macdonald to show his producer credentials and find a director. 'While I sweated out another new draft, Macdonald spent the next two months having lunch, which is apparently the accepted method of finding a director,' noted Hodge wryly.

Macdonald claims his search for someone to helm the film wasn't as relaxed as Hodge might have thought. 'We knew we wanted the sort of person who was about to make their name,' he claimed. 'We didn't want an established name or someone who had tried and failed. We wanted someone who was hot, and in some ways, our equivalent, but a more experienced film-maker.'

Macdonald's ultimate choice – after working through a shortlist of candidates – was Danny Boyle, previously best known for his acclaimed work for BBC TV on *Mr Wroe's Virgins*. Boyle had a strong track record of television and theatre direction and production, but there was nothing in his professional background in particular to suggest he was the ideal person for *Shallow Grave*. The snare for him was the script, as it had been for Allan Scott. 'I thought this was one of the most exciting scripts I'd read, because unlike most British writing for television or screen, it was very simple, very dynamic and didn't carry a lot of history or moral baggage with it.'

The other unique thing Boyle noticed about *Shallow Grave* was how modern and cosmopolitan the screenplay appeared – not at all stuck in the British costume drama tradition. 'Although its social milieu is very British, there was something "American" about its absolute concentration on the drive of the narrative – and a constantly surprising narrative at that – which makes for wonderful cinema.' For Macdonald, it was a match made in heaven. 'Danny immediately understood the script and the characters. He was undoubtedly the man.'

The producer and director now faced a key challenge – the casting. The first role was easy to fill. Boyle had worked with New Zealand actress Kerry Fox in *Mr Wroe's Virgins* and she'd been acclaimed for her work in Jane Campion's *An Angel at My Table* (1990), where she'd given a performance as author Janet Frame which critic Leonard Maltin had called 'riveting'. She was ideal for the role of Juliet, the trainee doctor among the three flatmates.

'I don't know if Juliet really feels that she's a puppeteer, but even in the hospital scenes, it's as if she only exists in relation to one of the boys,' Fox remembers of the pivotal role her character plays in balancing each of her male flatmates with the other. 'And so that's the way I worked on it too. I didn't make any decisions prior to pre-take rehearsals because I couldn't decide what to do until I had seen what the other two were doing, then I could pitch the balance somewhere. I found, however, during the scene when she's being interviewed by the police, that she enjoyed it. Once she is inside the flat with those boys, she gives herself the opportunity for anything to happen. It's like a game. She wants to play fantasies. Maybe this relates to John Hodge being a doctor himself and wanting to write a script which is his fantasy of allowing anything to happen'.

The two male leads – a buttoned-down accountant who cracks up and a cynical hack with a heart of gold – would be far harder to cast, given the film's budget. 'The two male leads I had in mind,' admitted Hodge, 'were Ray Liotta and Bill Murray!'

'I always thought it would be an interesting film, Danny's so clever and he's got a great eye.'

As with their choice of director, Macdonald and Hodge were looking for 'rising stars', actors with a bit of experience, who showed talent and perhaps would be capable of greater things in the future but would be cheap at the moment. Christopher Eccleston fitted the bill, having made an impact in *Let Him Have It* (1991), a drama about a miscarriage of justice, and a series of acclaimed stage and TV performances, including a regular character on *Cracker*.

'I wanted to avoid doing the Monty Python chartered accountant,' he said of his approach to his character in *Shallow Grave*. 'Every time Alex speaks to David, he puts him down, which suggests that Alex fears him or is unsettled by him. The thing about David is that, in a strange way, he finds a power, a self which was lacking, through doing this horrific thing. He's pushed and pushed into dismembering that corpse, but once he does it, he's achieved something. This square, quiet, put-upon guy has done something that these other two – who have the pretence of being dangerous – could never have done. He surprises himself and the other two by making a stand.'

The final piece of the casting jigsaw to fall into place was, arguably, the most important. The first choice for Alex was Scottish actor Robert Carlyle. Carlyle was interested – until Boyle asked him to tone down his 'working class' Scottish accent. 'I wanted to keep my accent,' Carlyle later told *The Scotsman* when outlining his reasons for turning down the part, 'not because I'm working class, but because it made more sense for the plot. I didn't think middle class people would be driven that far for the money. If you put it in a working class perspective, where people have got nothing, then there's a chance they might take that kind of risk.'

With Carlyle out of the picture, Boyle was forced to look elsewhere. He recalled hearing about Ewan McGregor from Ros Wolfes, the producer of *Mr Wroe's Virgins*. Wolfes had brought *Scarlet and Black* to the screen and had talked about how talented Ewan McGregor was. He was invited to meet with Boyle, Macdonald and Hodge. They all hit it off immediately and the production team knew they'd found their Alex Law.

The three flatmates in *Shallow Grave* are joined by a short-lived fourth, the mysterious Hugo (Keith Allen). He seems reclusive, and when he doesn't come out of his room for several days, the curious trio break in to discover not only his corpse, but a bag stuffed full of cash. Alex suggests they keep the money and dispose of the body, and goads the other two into carrying out the scheme.

For Ewan, the heart of his character was to be found in his surroundings. With so much of the action taking place in the flat itself, he drew on the restriction to get to understand his character: 'I think he feels so secure in this flat because he feels so insecure everywhere else.'

A six-week period of pre-production began late in summer 1993, including one week of rehearsals in Glasgow – an unusual approach to film-making. For director Danny Boyle it was the ideal way to

'Alex was openly aggressive and I'm not.
I'd suddenly be humiliating people at
parties. It was quite worrying.'

Above: Ewan with his Shallow Grave *co-stars Christopher Eccleston and Kerry Fox; they all moved into a flat together during the filming to build on their characters relationships.*

break the ice. 'I decided that rather than us just meeting in the rehearsal room and then going back to hotels or whatever, we should all move into a flat together. It was short-hand really, a way of getting to know people: and they did get to know each other very, very quickly. It surprised me how fast they bonded,' said Boyle of his trio of actors. 'I suppose they couldn't mess about – they were right on top of each other all the time, and all their habits – bad habits – were exposed to everybody straight away.'

For McGregor, this period of close contact with his co-stars was perfect. 'The most important thing about the film,' he said, 'is their relationship in the flat and the fact that they've lived together far too long. And that rehearsal period was brilliant from the word go. We used to get up, have breakfast and do scenes in our pyjamas. In a rehearsal room you'd set up chairs and tables, pretend there was a wall here and a door there; but we were in a real flat, so there *was* a wall there. It allowed us to get used to each other, at the same time as getting used to our characters.'

Meeting Christopher Eccleston and Kerry Fox for the first time and having to be downright rude and nasty to them – albeit in a charming way – was a challenge for Ewan. 'The only time you ever see him speaking to people he's being rude,' said the actor of Alex. 'The greed for money, the desire to get away with it, is very much in Alex because, up to that point, the others have let him get away with being king of the flat. The whole thing hinges on his yearning for Juliet; he wants her so badly – and that's a nice quality in him – that you quite like him and begin to see him as a bit of a loveable bastard.'

In preparation to play such an aggressive and argumentative character, Ewan drew inspiration from a surprising source – Scottish and American stand-up comedians, from Billy Connolly to Dennis Leary and little-known American comedy duo the Jerky Boys. He obtained tapes of their routines and based Alex's verbal style on their sharp wit and rapid-fire delivery. The incredulity in Alex's voice when a bag full of money falls into his lap, and his disbelief at the turn of events during the film, comes from listening intently to these routines.

'I had to find a way not to feel uncomfortable about being aggressive to people. Alex was openly aggressive and I'm not.' Ewan later felt he'd got into the character perhaps a little too deep. 'I'd suddenly be humiliating people at parties. It was quite worrying.'

'I've always found that actors who try to teach you how to do it are always the ones you don't want to learn from.'

For much of his TV work Ewan had been required to soften his accent and make his speech style somewhat blander, so he was glad of the opportunity that *Shallow Grave* gave him to speak as he sounds in real life. It was a move that wasn't without risk, as using his real voice allowed him nowhere to hide. 'It's weird to be doing something in my own accent because it makes me feel very naked. It's also the first thing that I've done in contemporary clothing, which is much harder, because I've got nothing to hide behind – no cravats, no English accent.'

Shallow Grave was shot in six weeks, with location work around Central Scotland. Among the location sites used in the film were the Royal Alexandria Hospital in Paisley, including the mortuary, the Georgian New Town of Edinburgh, where the flat was supposedly located, the newsroom of the *Evening Times* in Glasgow, where McGregor's character of Alex was supposed to work, and the forest in Rouken Glen near Glasgow, which provided a chilling night-time backdrop to gruesome scenes of digging graves and dissecting bodies.

The primary location, though, was to be the flat itself. Rather than shoot in a real location, the underfunded production team were set the task of creating a fantasy flat, supposedly located in Edinburgh, but built in make-shift studio facilities in Glasgow. Constructed slightly larger than life-size, the sets for the flat interior were erected in the warehouse on an industrial estate in Glasgow that was to serve as the studio base.

'What we always wanted was that it should be a flat worth dying for,' joked director Danny Boyle. 'It's a flat that stirs up feelings of slight envy about these people's lives, and so you want to join in with them and *be* them in a way. This flat shouldn't just be a place where they sleep; the whole world is in there. The characters have to go to work to earn money, but apart from that they appear to have no other life – only the flat and each other. People are not invited back; nobody's ever expected to come round; people ring up and are told to get lost, basically; the mail is carefully censored on its way in. It's a cocoon really, that they have made for themselves.'

While director of photography Brian Tufano and editor Masahiro Hirakubo were experienced professionals, many of the others on the set were relatively new to the film business and were drawn from a young, talented pool of Scottish technicians and actors.

'There are only about twenty cinema films made in the UK each year,' noted producer Andrew Macdonald, 'so, if you make one, that's an achievement in itself. In Scotland, *Shallow Grave* was the only cinema film made in 1993, which put a lot of pressure on us. Our predecessors were American independent films, that style of storytelling, but it's like old Hollywood too – something that's well-crafted. This was to be a young, hip, funny, contemporary Scottish thriller – slightly raw, slightly shocking – which, hopefully, made you laugh in some of the wrong places.'

Blatantly displaying Hodge's American influences, it revolves around the changing relationships of the central trio as the police close in on them. As for the performances, Ewan's wild, manic Alex dominated proceedings, with both Kerry Fox and Christopher Eccleston struggling hard to keep up. It makes for a breathtaking 90 minutes.

Like Ewan, Andrew Macdonald was not lacking in ambition and drive, and he put *Shallow Grave* up for selection in competition at the 1994 Cannes Film Festival. For once, he came unstuck. The film was refused, and so ended up being screened out of competition. However, it didn't matter that much to him – *Shallow Grave* might now not win any prizes, but a screening at Cannes was bound to secure some foreign distribution deals.

It was a sign of things to come that *Shallow Grave*, this quirky, low-budget, unassuming yet in-your-face thriller quickly became the talk of the Croissette. Such was the demand to see the film that Macdonald had to quickly arrange three extra screenings. The brash B-movie that the team behind *Shallow Grave* thought they had on their hands was quickly turning into something else.

Showbusiness bible *Variety* hailed the industry screenings, even going so far as to question why the film wasn't in competition. It called *Shallow Grave* 'a tar black comedy that zings along on a wave of visual and scripting inventiveness'. Inevitably, comparisons were made between *Shallow Grave* and the early work of the Coen Brothers – particularly *Blood Simple* – especially as their latest film, *The Hudsucker Proxy*, had opened that year's Festival.

The hype surrounding the film continued to build from its debut at Cannes in May 1994 to its UK-wide release in January 1995. By then, Macdonald, Hodge and Boyle were being hailed as the latest saviours of the almost-always ailing British film industry, the film was being compared commercially to *Four Weddings and a Funeral*, and Ewan McGregor found himself being hailed as one of the fastest-rising and most talented stars of his generation.

Shallow Grave took just over £5 million in the UK, making it the biggest British film of the year. It smashed the house records at five London cinemas over the opening weekend, including the MGM Haymarket and Gate Cinema in Notting Hill. The film would go on to take £20 million world-wide. For Angus Wolfe Murray, then film critic of *The Scotsman*, Ewan McGregor was 'quite wonderful', and part of a superb ensemble cast who were 'perfectly matched'.

Although he was acclaimed in the press and enjoying his biggest success yet, offscreen Ewan's life had taken something of a downturn. During the making of *Shallow Grave* he'd split up with Marie Pairis. Back in London and single once more, he claimed he was set to enjoy his life once again. 'I have no time for women at the moment,' he'd claimed in an interview with the *Mail on Sunday*. 'There's nothing on the cards and I'm quite happy.'

In January 1994, just after he'd wrapped on *Shallow Grave*, Ewan had won a role in the two-hour pilot film for a Carlton Television legal drama, *Kavanagh QC*, which was to be broadcast a year later. His part was of a student, David Armstrong, who was accused of raping middle-aged housewife Eve Kendall (played by Alison Steadman). It was not the most glamorous role.

Working on the series was Eve Mavrakis, a French production designer. It was love at first sight between them, despite the circumstances. 'How very romantic,' Ewan acknowledged. 'Eve was sitting upstairs and I was raping Alison Steadman downstairs. She says she can remember sitting upstairs and listening to us. It was fantastic. She's a brilliant woman.'

Eve was five years older than Ewan, having been born in June 1966 in the Dordogne in France. Among the films she worked on were Steven Spielberg's *Empire of the Sun*, and the acclaimed *Bandit Queen*, which had brought her to London in the early nineties.

The relationship developed quickly but discreetly. Soon Eve had moved in with McGregor and they were laying plans to get married. Before that could happen, though, Ewan had several projects to complete – one of which would reunite him with the *Shallow Grave* team.

CHAPTER 4

SURFING THE WAVE

EWAN McGREGOR IS NOT A LAZY MAN. From the beginning of his film career with *Shallow Grave*, he has not stopped. Early in 1994 he'd completed *Kavanagh QC* and met Eve Mavrakis, but he didn't settle down to an instant domestic life. There were other challenges, other roles out there waiting for him. He knew, before it had opened, that he'd done good work in *Shallow Grave*. The question he tormented himself with over and over again was: could he continue to do it?

He got his chance to perform again in a BBC TV film called *Doggin' Around*. Produced by Ariel Productions from a script by Alan Plater and directed by Desmond Davis, this one-off production was transmitted in October 1994. It featured a rare UK TV appearance by American actor Elliot Gould in the leading role of ageing American jazz musician Joe Warren, an alcoholic, gambler and womaniser, who has come to the North of England to play a series of gigs. There he meets the woman who is to be his minder for the week and realises that the consequences of the last visit he had made to the same place ten years before have finally caught up with him.

The Northern trip is forced upon Warren when a gig at Ronnie Scott's London jazz club is cancelled – Scott even appeared as himself, alongside a cast which included Geraldine James, Alun Armstrong, Liz Smith and Judy Flynn. McGregor played one of the band who accompany Joe Warren up north. *Doggin' Around* was not to be a major achievement in Ewan's developing career, but he had higher hopes for his next film.

Like the genesis of *Shallow Grave*, *Blue Juice* started with a meeting between two cinematic enthusiasts who'd never made a feature film before. While at the Royal College of Art, Peter Salmi and Carl Prechezer had started working together with the simple intention of producing straightforwardly entertaining material – quality films that would appeal to a mainstream audience. In that respect, the maverick pair were at pains to distinguish themselves from the rest of Britain's 'art house' film producers. They were in it for the fun – how else could they have conceived of a surfing drama set in Cornwall?

The pair had produced some shorts while at college and these had come to the attention of Simon Relph, one of the movers and shakers in the British film industry, a leading film producer whose work had included *Damage*, *Camilla* and *The Secret Rapture*. Suspecting that Salmi and Prechezer had the right approach and might go on to produce some mainstream movie hits, he invited them to work with his film production company, Skreba.

The first result of this collaboration was a short for Channel 4's Short and Curlies strand, an outlet for television screening of short films. Their work *The Cutter*, produced by Relph, was based on their own script, produced by Salmi and directed by Prechezer. The short was distributed in cinemas alongside Louis Malle's *Damage* before its television screening in January 1994. The previous year it had won the Silver Plaque at the Chicago International Film Festival. This success – and a second short called *Dirtysomething* – gave Relph enough confidence in his protégés to have them produce a feature film.

'*The Cutter* is actually about a dysfunctional relationship between a father and son,' explained Salmi. 'It could be very boring set in a room in Hackney. The father is a contract killer, the boy wants to follow in his footsteps but is the worst person in the world to do that. Now that is immediately a high concept idea. It's entertaining because of the high drama it contains and underneath it is those ideas. *Dirtysomething* is the story of a romance falling apart. We set it in the context of travellers getting sucked up into a world of home improvement and DIY.'

Keen on their pitch for an offbeat, whimsical and mystical comedy drama set amongst the vibrant Cornish surfing scene (the title refers to the way surfers see the sea), Relph put Salmi and

Prechezer in touch with David Aukin at Channel 4 – the man who'd been instrumental in giving the green light to *Shallow Grave* and would later back *Trainspotting*. As Head of Drama at the station, Aukin was one of the few individuals in the British film industry who could get a film underway simply by agreeing to back it. He commissioned a screenplay from Salmi and Prechezer.

According to Salmi, the choice of subject matter wasn't as offbeat as it might have seemed. 'For our debut feature, Carl and I wanted to make a character-driven comedy about life for the late-twenties generation in Britain today,' he claimed. 'We wanted a setting that would give a rollercoaster ride along the way.'

'I had a great time filming in Cornwall for ten weeks, I've never partied so much in my life.'

It was this search for a unique milieu for their comedy-drama that brought the pair to the little-known British surfing community. 'An old friend of mine, Tim, started to go out with a girl who was originally in Cornwall, went there for the weekend, spent the week, came back and said, "You've got to go down, check this out",' remembered Prechezer. 'I think the thing that he reacted to apart from the surfing, apart from the fact that when the waves happen, whole towns clear out and charge into the water, was the people, the music scene, the clothes, everything. There's a whole culture that he was attracted to.'

Prechezer felt that this community would be the ideal setting for their twentysomething drama – it was British, unusual and could be very visual. 'We had wanted for a long time to make a film about a younger group of people, people who were in our age group,' said Prechezer, agreeing with Salmi. 'We didn't have a setting for it. When Tim came back, we just thought this would be the perfect place to set a film like that. All the people that we knew, all the characters that we knew, were from London and so the story started to develop as the story of a London guy who goes there and gets into surfing.'

As potential producer, Salmi was keen to ensure that the locations were as promising in reality as they'd been in Tim's stories. 'We visited Cornwall and discovered a home-grown surfing scene. The script described the location as "sun-kissed sands, Cornwall at its best". The reality was slate-grey skies.'

The unusual idea of surfing in Britain seemed to tickle people's fancy. 'That's the joke of it, the comedy of it,' explained Prechezer. 'You say to people, "We're making a British surf film," and most people's reaction is, "People surf in this country?" Also there's a lot of irony there: people expect surfing to be on some sun-kissed beach somewhere, whereas it's not like that at all in this country. It's the first British surf movie and it's a good hook in a sense. When people start to hear more about the project, they realise that there's more to it than just surfing. We're not really a surf movie. We don't follow a group of surfers about the place as they search for the perfect wave.'

To chronicle the misadventures of a quartet of twenty-something lads, Salmi and Prechezer needed the right cast to bring their characters to life. They pulled together four of the hippest young actors in Britain – Sean Pertwee (son of the late Jon Pertwee, the third Doctor Who), Steven Mackintosh, Peter Gunn and, of course, Ewan McGregor, for whom this £2 million production would be his biggest-budgeted film yet. *Blue Juice* also attracted Catherine Zeta Jones as the surf king's love interest. For Prechezer, this was the right line up of new, young British talent who were just beginning to be noticed. 'People are starting to be aware of the cast, with Catherine Zeta Jones, who a lot of people have seen and liked a lot on television, Sean Pertwee who's started to get a lot of notoriety because of *Shopping*, and Ewan McGregor through *Shallow Grave*.'

Ewan had high expectations of the film, even though he wasn't playing a leading role, but, while he thoroughly enjoyed shooting it, he was somewhat disappointed by the outcome. 'I had a great time filming in Cornwall for ten weeks,' he told *Details* about the September to November 1994 shoot on *Blue Juice*. 'I've never partied so much in my life. The film's a good laugh. I mean, it's a bit muddled in the middle. It's just a shame – it's not really very good.'

Part of the problem might have been Ewan's focus on having a good time rather than producing a good performance. He claims to recall one night's heavy drinking when he and his pals thought their chauffeur had come to join them, until they realised that it was in fact morning and he'd come to ferry them to the location for a day's shooting. Luckily, Ewan was able to spend most of the day hiding behind a pair of sunglasses. 'It really doesn't make you feel very clever,' he claimed about his misdemeanour. 'I haven't done it since – he lies!'

This desire to have fun and get drunk was to impact on other films Ewan was to make, with his hangover becoming not only a feature of his early-morning on-set appearances, but also constantly referred to in his interviews, as he'd often be nursing one when chatting to a reporter. 'I love a pint,' he boasted. 'I love loads of them! You know when you've got a hangover and you really look for sausages and mash, or steak and kidney pie and chips? I love all that stodge, it's great.'

The four leading actors had to be able to convince on film that they were surfers. In preparation, they worked under the tutelage of two of the best surfers in the UK, Rob Small and Steve England, who also found themselves press-ganged by the film crew into acting as surfing doubles for the leading men. Sean Pertwee, whose role demanded more obvious surfing skill than those of his co-stars, made some early trips to Cornwall in order to get ahead with the lessons and soon became quite accomplished at the sport, albeit not a fan of the low sea temperatures off Britain's coastline.

'Sean revelled in his surf training,' recalled Salmi of his leading man's endeavours. 'His progress astonished his instructor, who proclaimed that Sean was just one step away from jacking in his acting career to become a full time surf bum, news that would have delighted Sean's agent!'

With Prechezer behind the camera, shooting began on 26 September 1994 on location. The dramatic coastal scenery and the picturesque harbour towns provided a host of choices for impressive visuals. It was also an appropriately contradictory backdrop to the colourful and garish attire of the would-be surf kings, their outfits being more suited to California than England.

Although both Salmi and Prechezer had the experienced Simon Relph on hand as a producer, they were keen to make their mark with a minimum of hand-holding. With a budget of £2 million, Salmi had to make sure that schedules were adhered to and the shooting timetable didn't slip.

For production designer Mark Tildesley, *Blue Juice* was a constant challenge to make the most of limited resources and even more limited shooting time. 'The budget and the resources weren't ideal,' he admitted. 'I suppose the most challenging thing was to try and get the thing to look right, to look like Cornwall. We had to go down there and spend time looking, researching the style, the music. And then trying to achieve things in the weather conditions: it's very difficult to film things in the harbour when you're expecting a gale force wind. But it was good fun. We had to try and improvise things as the film went on. In the end some of the shots were done by strapping someone like Ewan McGregor to the back of a flatbed truck with water splashing up in their face. It was simply easier.'

'I love a pint, I love loads of them!'

Salmi recalled how they learned of the problems filming at sea on the first day's shooting. 'Half an hour after lunch, the local lifeboat was on standby, a valuable piece of equipment had been destroyed by salt water and we lurched back through the turbulent ocean to the safety of the harbour. Carl and I then contemplated changing the focus of the film, from surfing to crazy golf.'

The cheerful nature of the sometimes arduous shoot was on display on the third day when Allon Reich, the Deputy Head of Drama at Channel 4, paid a visit to the location to keep an eye on proceedings. 'I took him to the boat,' recalled Salmi, 'to find Ewan, Sean and Peter [Gunn] screaming "I love this job". They'd had a great day filming, the dolphins had swum with them and it was a wonderful moment for our financiers to understand the vibe the film was being made with.'

At the end of the week that was given over to Cornwall, the cast and crew relocated for further shooting, mainly of indoor studio-based scenes at Pinewood Studios. Then a lucky few went on with a reduced crew to a fortnight's filming in Lanzarote in the Canary Islands. Many of Sean Pertwee's surf board scenes were completed in these more hospitable waters.

As if in payback for his earlier inattention to his role, Ewan was struck down by a bug late in filming. Producer Peter Salmi believed he'd caught something nasty from the waters around Cornwall. His illness didn't last long, and Eve had to comfort him as she made frequent visits to the location shooting and became well known to the cast and crew. It was clear to all who saw them together that the couple were very serious about one another.

Above: Ewan McGregor with Anthony Etherton in Doggin Around.
Below: Ewan and Vivian Wu in Peter Greenaway's erotic study of desire and obsession in The Pillow Book.

When it finally appeared, *Blue Juice* was not well received, with Angus Wolfe Murray in *The Scotsman* going so far as to claim that both Catherine Zeta Jones and Ewan McGregor were 'wasted' in the film. The box office take in the UK was only £256,000, while in North America the *Toronto Sun's* critic Bruce Kirkland was to complain: 'Despite a gonzo performance by Trainspotter Ewan McGregor, *Blue Juice* doesn't measure up. The surf may be up, but *Blue Juice* is a washout.' *Eye Weekly* dubbed the Film 'a tedious, failed comedy . . . a feeble imitation of *Baywatch* . . . dull and predictable even by TV standards'.

His next film would see Ewan working with one of the more idiosyncratic talents of contemporary British film-making. Peter Greenaway has proved to be a striking, sometimes

'People say Greenaway treats actors like flowerpots. It's true he doesn't direct you much but, once I got used to it, there was a wonderful freedom in that.'

controversial but always provocative figure. Trained as a painter – a background which repeatedly shows up in his films – Greenaway began work as a film editor in 1965 for the government's Central Office of Information. He spent eleven years editing public information films, and certainly some of the later ones show signs of the trademarks he would develop more fully in his feature film work, such as rhythmic editing, obsessive list-making and colour coding.

Although he has continued to produce paintings and has curated a number of exhibitions, as well as exhibited his own work, it is as an artistic film-maker that Greenaway is best known. From his first feature film, *The Draughtman's Contract* in 1982, through controversial work such as *A Zed and Two Noughts* (1986), *The Cook, the Thief, His Wife and Her Lover* (1989) to *The Baby of Macon* (1993), Greenaway has established an international reputation as one of Europe's most original film-makers.

Having worked with Ralph Fiennes and Julia Ormond on *The Baby of Macon* before both became internationally known movie stars, Greenaway – for all his art house leanings – has shown an eye for spotting rising acting talent. That was certainly the case when he recruited Ewan to take a leading role in his 1995 study of desire and obsession, *The Pillow Book*.

'The Pillow Book was based on a notion that the most important things in life are physicality and literature,' Greenaway has said. 'Metaphors and images in the film are constantly about the stimulations of flesh and text. The narrative concerns an emancipated woman with a love of literature who likes her lovers to write on her body. The text on the body is not permanent – there are no notions of branding and tattooing. That makes an association with the ephemerality of the flesh – connections between the mortality of paper and flesh and writing.'

The original 'pillow book' which inspired Greenaway's film was written by a female member of the Japanese imperial court during the Heian period (794-1185), called Sei Shonagon. The 'book' was no more than a collection of memories, lists, quotes from other texts which had caught the author's eye, and tales of life and love. The style and content of this pillow book, linking explicit text with sex, echoed many of the concerns which Greenaway had already tackled in films like *Prospero's Books* (1991), a fabulous retelling of Shakespeare's *The Tempest* with Sir John Gielgud, and his eight-part 1989 *ATV Dante* series.

The film spans from the seventies to the end of the twentieth century, chronicling the erotic adventures of Kyoto-born Nagiko (Vivian Wu). Nagiko's fetish dates back to her childhood birthdays, when her father (Ken Ogata) would carefully inscribe a birthday greeting on her face as her mother read from the book of the film's title. The driving story of the film is her search for a calligrapher-lover who can replicate her father's touch, giving the whole thing something of a oedipal tinge. She fails to find satisfaction until she meets Jerome (Ewan), a bisexual English translator.

He convinces her to use his body as a medium for her own writings, leading to a brief sexual liaison between the pair. Wishing to further Nagiko's writing ambitions, Jerome presents himself to her father's old publisher (Yoshi Oida). Soon Jerome is involved in a gay affair with the publisher, while Nagiko pursues her desire to write on skin and to be written on with other men. In an effort to win her back Jerome (in an echo of *Romeo and Juliet*) fakes suicide – which accidentally results in his real death. In her grief, Nagiko writes an erotic poem on his body before burying it. However, the publisher exhumes Jerome's corpse, flays the skin and has Nagiko's poem made into a pillow book for himself. The remainder of the film charts Nagiko's attempts to win back the book made of her lover's skin. The gruesome finale of *The Pillow Book* is a clear retelling of the climax of Greenaway's own *The Cook, the Thief, His Wife and Her Lover*, in which Michael Gambon's overbearing gangster is forced at gun point to eat the cooked corpse of his wife's lover.

For Ewan the role of Jerome was to be the most challenging of his career to date, although – as he was to discover – Peter Greenaway was not known for his overly sympathetic handling of his actors. 'From the moment I picked up the script and couldn't stop reading it, to the last day of filming, I thought it was the most beautiful story,' Ewan claimed of Greenaway's lurid melodrama. 'I was scared to begin with, but I think you do your most interesting work when you're not sure how it will work out. I'm into that.' He was pretty much on his own with the script when it came to bringing the character to life. 'Jerome is a complex and vain man. He shamelessly uses and manipulates the publisher, and really surprises himself when he falls madly in love with Nagiko (Vivian Wu). Generally not one to lose control, he starts off with a hopelessly romantic idea of his suicide.'

'From the moment I picked up the script and couldn't stop reading it, to the last day of filming, I thought it was the most beautiful story.'

'People say Greenaway treats actors like flowerpots,' Ewan confirmed of his director's reputation, during an interview at his London home after filming. 'It's true he doesn't direct you much but, once I got used to it, there was a wonderful freedom in that. He does these big, long, wide-shots and you get to just act your socks off.'

Ewan was nonetheless interested in the processes through which Greenaway went to capture his vision on film. 'Greenaway really is an artist. He paints with the camera. They light it and then he'll go and adjust things around the set as if he was about to sit down and paint them. You're as important as the leaves on the tree in the background. A lot of it was hand-held, which surprised me.'

The demands of the role, which involved spending most of the early part of 1995 shooting in Luxembourg, were unique in Ewan's career. 'This was a very different experience for me,' he confirmed. 'I found it very stimulating. I would regularly spend between two and four hours having calligraphy applied all over my body – very sensual, and something I will not forget in a long while.' The process involved an early morning wake-up call at about four a.m.

Peter Greenaway was instrumental in selecting the texts for each body himself – although British audiences would, for the most part, be unable to read the Japanese characters. Some of the texts he wrote himself, while others were drawn from Sei Shonagon. Sketches on paper were often followed by trials on life-size mannequins. When Ewan himself was ready for writing upon, his body was first marked off and gridded in white pencil. A full book, covering the entire body, would take three to four hours to complete.

One of the books inscribed on Ewan – book six, The Book of the Lover, written by Greenaway himself – was made up of 24-carat gold leaf glued to the actor's skin, making it glisten and – in the fiction of the film – giving the book and body intrinsic value.

It was his work on *The Pillow Book* that first gave Ewan the reputation for not being shy about stepping out of his clothes on film, although he also had to be naked every night in the Joe Orton play *What the Butler Saw*. 'Well, I think that's fucking great,' came the characteristic answer to the suggestion that some audience members were attending just to glimpse his nakedness. 'More people are going to see a piece of art, and if it takes my nadgers to get them in there, then all's the better.'

One problem Ewan had to get used to was the early morning temperature of the studio and of the ink used to inscribe the characters on his body. 'The ink was cold, because it's just so cold in Luxembourg, but once you get over that it's quite soothing and sensual,' he happily admitted. 'It took about four and a half hours to do the full front and back, so I'd arrive about half [past] four in the morning. They'd have a camp bed set up and a couple of heaters each side. I'd sleep for the first two hours on my back while they painted my front. And then I'd have to stand up for the two and a half hours while they did my back, which was less enjoyable and slightly more boring. I'd often get the Japanese extras to read me so I knew what I said. It was a surreal experience.'

Dropping his clothes would later become a regular feature of Ewan's on-screen life, so much so that he joked he'd had it written into his contracts. Later, when married to Eve, he would have

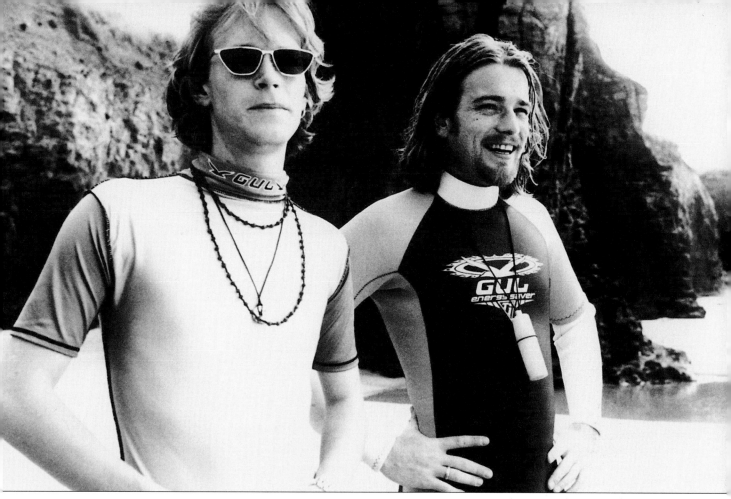

Above: Expecting sun-kissed sands, the cast and crew of Blue Juice *were faced with the slate-grey skies of Cornwall.*

second thoughts about his enthusiasm for going naked and enthusiastically indulging in on-screen sex. 'It's not easy for her to see things like that,' he admitted. 'I know I wouldn't like watching her boff someone else on screen. You have to be very careful with each other about that kind of thing, because it hurts. Keep it professional, or keep it in your pants – if you've got any on.'

Some time was spent filming on location in Japan (mainly for historical scenes set in the Heian period and the time of Nagiko's youth in the seventies) and Hong Kong (where the story switches after Nagiko leaves home, and where Jerome's fate is played out).

As the film spanned the last 30 years of the century, it involved Greenaway, McGregor and his costume and production designers in suggesting a possible look for the end of the century when the film reaches its climax. 'For the scenes set in the future,' noted costume designer Dien Van Straalen, 'the temptation was to draw on the sixties vision of ultra modern clothes – plastics and metallic fibres – but in fact the trend now is towards more natural materials. Ewan McGregor's character wears mainly Paul Smith, while with Vivian Wu it was very important that she come across as a successful high fashion model, but also look relaxed in her clothes.'

When released, *The Pillow Book* received a mixed critical reception. *The Scotsman* noted that Ewan was 'ill-at-ease as *l'objet d'amour*', while American critics like Janet Maslin of *the New York Times* were more welcoming: 'Jerome is played with charming insouciance by Ewan McGregor in what is sure to be a classic before-I-was-famous turn . . .' Ruthe Stein in the *San Francisco Chronicle* thought McGregor played 'the bisexual Jerome completely straight; he might have been more convincing with a lighter touch'. It appeared that Ewan's attempts to direct himself hadn't come off altogether successfully.

Production had wrapped on *The Pillow Book* early in 1995. There was no time for Ewan to rest, though, as he was about to enter one of the busiest periods of his life – both professionally and personally. By his 24th birthday on 31 March 1995 he'd been confirmed in the role of Mark Renton in *Trainspotting*, in a reunion with the creative team behind *Shallow Grave*. By the summer of 1995 he'd have married Eve Mavrakis – in a wedding ceremony held in France in a brief window between films – and by early 1996 he'd be celebrating the birth of a baby daughter. Ewan McGregor's life less ordinary was just about to begin.

CHAPTER 5

CHOOSE LIFE

IT HAD SEEMED CERTAIN THAT EWAN WOULD WORK AGAIN with Andrew Macdonald, John Hodge and Danny Boyle. As early as the completion of *Shallow Grave* he'd expressed just such a desire.

Just months after the short, sharp shoot for *Shallow Grave* was finished, Andrew Macdonald had turned his thoughts to the next project the team could tackle. On a flight from Glasgow to London he'd bumped into an old school friend who raved about a book she'd been reading, *Trainspotting* by Irvine Welsh. 'She described it in such enthusiastic terms that I immediately went to the book shop and bought a copy. I'm not a great reader – I don't read many novels at all – but I was really bowled over by this book, it was so powerful, uncompromising and, I felt, truthful and insightful about a certain section of British society. It was about a bunch of people – drug addicts, thieves, psychos and no-hopers – who don't usually get represented in fiction. There was such a raw quality to the writing, it really felt like it was written in a completely unsentimental way. What also appealed was the surrealistic style of it, the way it refuses to conform to social realism – which as a genre is one of my pet hates.'

In February 1994 Macdonald dropped off a copy of Irvine Welsh's controversial best-seller with John Hodge. 'I took the book, read it and, suitably stunned, I handed it back,' said Hodge of his first exposure to Welsh's episodic tale of the highs and lows of junkie life in Edinburgh's deprived housing estates.

'*Trainspotting* is an incredible book: its characters, language, narratives were like nothing I'd ever read before. I then explained to Andrew Macdonald why *Trainspotting* could never be made into a film.'

The first stumbling block that put Hodge on the defensive was the fact that the book was a collection of only loosely collected short stories, lacking a cohesive narrative link. Then the characters were largely defined through their interior monologues rather than dialogue. To put Macdonald off Hodge even resorted to claiming that he had in fact 'retired' from screenwriting. The task just seemed impossible.

However, Macdonald had been quick to learn the ropes of film production on *Shallow Grave*, and as he began the process of making *Trainspotting* he was quick to apply those lessons. He tempted Hodge back to the fold by hinting that there might be a bigger pay-day for the writer this time around. 'I re-read *Trainspotting*,' said Hodge, suitably mollified by the temptation of filthy lucre. 'I enjoyed it even more, noting the depth and humanity that I had missed first time around, having been dazzled then by the language and horror. I still didn't see it as a film, though. Boyle and Macdonald were not put off by my protests about the practical difficulties.'

A fortnight-long 'brainstorming' session was held several months later during 1994, with the trio breaking down the plot of *Trainspotting* into a series of discrete scenes, choosing what to include, what to lose and what had to be invented to thread the story together into a narrative suitable for a feature film. 'My intention was to produce a screenplay which would seem to have, approximately, a beginning, a middle and an end and would last 90 minutes and would convey at least some of the spirit and content of the book,' said Hodge about his ambition.

The process was a struggle, with Hodge having to amalgamate some of the characters, switch some incidents around and move them from one character to another, developing major scenes from minor details in the book (like the film's opening shoplifting sequence). There were also some things he had to create simply in order to bring dramatic cohesion to the screenplay. 'The easiest

'In a way, the movie's very much like heroin, it lets you laugh and takes you on a trip. Then doesn't really let you have such a good time anymore.'

decision was choosing a leading character,' said Hodge. 'Mark Renton is the book's strongest voice. He is honest, vitriolic, full of loathing and self-loathing, and is touched at moments by painful compassion. Once this journey was in place, the other characters were structured around him.'

To help develop the concept the trio took a trip to Leith in Edinburgh where the book was set. 'We did a lot of research among present-day heroin users in and around Edinburgh,' remembered Boyle, who was preparing to direct the film. 'It was a really grim, depressing experience, one which we were all immediately familiar with from so many social realist TV dramas and public health warnings, where the people are absolute victims. What we realised was that Irvine Welsh's book was not about that kind of environment. He acknowledges that terrible, destructive side of drugs, but his particular characters – the central ones – are not victims. Welsh was dealing with a much more seductive and sensual area – he asks about the attractions of heroin.'

During the research, the trio discovered the Calton Athletic Drug Rehabilitation Centre in Glasgow. Here they found a group of former addicts – seen among the football team at the beginning of the film – who had overcome the drug, just like the characters in the book. 'They were a great inspiration to us,' Macdonald claimed of the group. 'Not only in an abstract way, they also became our guides through the drug culture, explaining and demonstrating for us.'

Securing the film rights to the novel proved to be a problem, as they had already been sold by publisher Minerva to Noel Gay TV, who had no plans to produce a film. As soon as they realised that Macdonald and co were interested, Noel Gay TV demanded to be co-producers, a development that Macdonald was not at all happy about. However, despite the failure to secure the rights at this stage, Hodge was instructed by Macdonald to continue writing.

'What a birthday present of a part! Renton really appealed to me. I imagined myself doing the work, and it felt good.'

At the same time, the threesome had turned down an approach by Hollywood producer Scott Rudin (*Sabrina*, *The Firm*) who offered $250,000 for them to develop any project they liked. After the showing of *Shallow Grave* at Cannes, Hollywood was beginning to show an interest in the creative team behind the movie, but Macdonald, Boyle and Hodge were not about to jump at the first offer to relocate to America. All three were committed to bringing Welsh's book to the screen. 'They said we were crazy to do a drug movie,' recalled Boyle of the contacts the team had with Hollywood. 'They'd say: "Why don't you do a thriller with Sharon Stone?"'

By November 1994 John Hodge had completed a 40-page draft of the first half of the film. 'I remember reading it coming back on the tube,' said Boyle of his first sight of Hodge's work, 'and I just roared with laughter. The feel of the book is surrealistic and he'd captured the tone brilliantly.'

Over Christmas and into the early months of 1995 – just as *Shallow Grave* was released in the UK and was making a big splash – Hodge developed a second draft, which went to Channel 4 in February 1995. 'I felt a certain loyalty to them,' declared producer Andrew Macdonald. 'They believed in *Shallow Grave* when nobody else did and were so great to work with right through the production, even through a few tricky spots we had. I also felt that *Trainspotting* was a specialist film – it was never going to be *Terminator 2* – and quite a difficult subject, and Channel 4 was the perfect place to take it. A big Hollywood studio wouldn't have touched it – or if they had, they would have made us change it beyond recognition. At Channel 4 we got to make the film that we wanted – as long as we kept the budget down.'

Channel 4 agreed to fund the entire film to the tune of £1.5 million, £500,000 more than the budget for *Shallow Grave*, but they wouldn't release a penny until the difficulties over the screen rights for the book had been resolved. With Irvine Welsh as well as Channel 4 by now on their side, Macdonald, Hodge and Boyle were able to resolve the problem by April 1995, with Noel Gay TV taking no active role in the production but accepting a percentage share of any profits and a name check on the credits.

By spring 1995 everything was in place and pre-production could begin. First thing on the agenda was casting the central role of Mark Renton, but the only name considered was Ewan's. He had just wrapped filming on *The Pillow Book*, and was confirmed in the role around his 24th birthday. 'What a birthday present of a part! Renton really appealed to me. I imagined myself doing the work, and it felt good,' enthused Ewan, despite having to shave his head and lose 30 pounds for the role. 'I just stopped drinking beer, really.'

Ewan had known for a while that the *Shallow Grave* team were endeavouring to mount a film version of *Trainspotting* and that chances were he'd be in it somewhere. He'd duly read Welsh's novel to get a handle on his character, while he waited for John Hodge to complete the screenplay. 'I liked his ballsy courage and intelligence,' he said of Mark Renton. 'There's something exciting about someone that nihilistic.'

Like Jerome in *The Pillow Book*, Renton seemed like a once-in-a lifetime opportunity – but then, the speed with which Ewan makes films, that could apply practically to any part that snares his interest. 'It was the kind of part you don't read very often and it was exactly the part that I personally felt I wanted to play at the time. I was looking for the part of Mark Renton – and there it was. There's a lot of him that just goes along passively with what everybody else is doing. Renton is most often observing. In a lot of scenes I don't have a lot to do physically, but at the same time he almost always has a critical edge about things in his mind, which is expressed in the voice-over which runs quite extensively through the film. Renton is the kind of person who ends an argument by saying, "Oh well, it's all shite anyway." If he can't come to a conclusion, he'll just dismiss everything.'

Ewan realised the part would entail a lot of research to accurately portray a drug abuser who's trying to escape the life he's leading. He even discussed with director Danny Boyle whether he should try shooting heroin – all in the interest of realism. After much consideration and after embarking on a series of meetings with recovering addicts, he decided to steer well clear of the idea. 'I thought about it,' he admitted candidly, 'and the more research I did, the less I wanted to do it. I don't think it's necessary. I've had to die on screen before and I don't know what that's like either. I'm not a method actor at all, so to take heroin for the part would just be an excuse to take heroin, really. It's a matter of taking what you've heard and read, and recreating that.'

It's possible that Ewan may have had more of an insight into the nature of addictive personalities than he himself understood. In one interview he was emphatic about his aversion to drugs – but notably excluded alcohol. 'No, no, no, not at all,' he reacted when asked if he'd taken heroin himself. 'Booze, lots of booze, but that was it. I wasn't involved in the rave scene when it kicked off in the eighties. I can't remember where I was, but I wasn't there! I've never been in a drugs scene at all.'

In fact, his drinking had grown steadily along with his fame. Admitting a liking of 'extremes' he was on a road which might have followed that of one of his favourite actors, Richard Burton, if he hadn't met and married Eve Mavrakis. It was this aspect of his personality that made him the ideal actor to tackle the role of Mark Renton, because he knew where Renton was coming from.

'In a way, the movie's very much like heroin,' he noted. 'It lets you laugh and takes you on this trip. Then it doesn't really let you have such a good time anymore. Listening to addicts talk at their meetings, I lost any sort of romantic curiosity for the drug. I couldn't have played Renton feeling like that.'

'I've never been in a drugs scene at all.'

Ewan immersed himself in books on the subject of the attraction and addiction of drugs. 'I read all the books I could get hold of on the subject, then during the two weeks' rehearsal before we started shooting, Danny got all sorts of people, mostly ex-heroin addicts, to come in and talk to us about it. Even prior to that, when I was on the Peter Greenaway film *The Pillow Book* in Luxembourg, I used to go to the train station on Sundays and hang around all day watching this really obvious group of junkies who congregated there. I got some of my look from them and some physical ideas. For instance, in one of the first scenes I used this particular stooped posture for Renton which is an exact rip-off of a guy I saw in Luxembourg.'

He was also glad to be back as part of the team. 'I was just really looking forward to coming back up to Scotland,' he said after his work in Cornwall and Luxembourg. 'We sort of picked up where we left off. In some ways it's been much easier because Danny and I have developed a short-hand way of communicating between us. But in other ways it's been more of a slog for me. I'm on set from morning to night, virtually every day because I'm in so many scenes. I only had one day off during the shoot.'

As *Trainspotting* was to be as much of an ensemble production as *Shallow Grave*, Danny Boyle had several other major roles in the film to cast. 'We made a list of the top talent. We saw a lot of

Above: To play the part of Renton in Trainspotting, *Ewan had to shave his head and lose 30 pounds.*

'I'm not a method actor at all, so to take heroin for the part would just be an excuse to take heroin, really. It's a matter of taking what you've heard and read, and recreating that.'

actors, some of whom we recognised from casting *Shallow Grave*. For some of the parts we knew who we wanted – people like Ewen Bremner [as Spud] and Bobby Carlyle [as Begbie].'

Boyle thought they may have a problem with Ewen Bremner as he had been playing the role of Renton in a stage adaptation of *Trainspotting* at London's Bush Theatre. He also thought Carlyle might hold a grudge after failing to win the role of Alex in *Shallow Grave*. It came as a relief when both of them accepted their roles, despite neither being the starring part. 'We wondered whether they would consider playing parts that were "beneath them", especially Ewen Bremner, but getting them to agree to play Spud and Begbie was a huge boost.'

The rest of the main cast were made up of Kevin McKidd, who'd appeared in Gilles McKinnon's *Small Faces*, Johnny Lee Miller, later to feature in *Regeneration*, *Hackers*, *Gattaca* and Alan Rudolph's *Afterglow*, as Sick Boy, and Kelly MacDonald, picked from hundreds who came to an open audition for the role, as Diane, Renton's schoolgirl one-night stand. 'I knew straight away before she even sat down and opened her mouth that she was the one,' Boyle recalled. Boyle also found small roles for *Shallow Grave* stalwarts Keith Allen and Peter Mullan (who was to win an acting award at the 1998 Cannes Film Festival for Ken Loach's *My Name is Joe*, which was also made in Glasgow).

Macdonald decided to shoot the film in Glasgow, like *Shallow Grave*, despite its Edinburgh setting. He managed to gain access to the disused Wills Cigarette Factory on Alexandra Parade, which once employed 5,000 people, as a production base and studio facility. Macdonald found that the factory's attributes were ideal for the film: 'It's an enormous place on two floors. There was enough room to build as many sets as we wanted, but we made use of the factory's old social club to double as a pub in the film.'

'Listening to addicts talk at their meetings, I lost any sort of romantic curiosity for the drug . . .

With an optimistic ending now attached to the screenplay, production was ready to commence in May 1995. The crew assembled while the actors started rehearsing in the second week of May at the top of one of Glasgow's distinctive tower blocks. Wishing to reunite as many of the *Shallow Grave* crew as possible, Boyle recruited Brian Tufano as director of photography, Kave Quinn as production designer and Masahiro Hirakubo as editor. Quinn was immediately set the task of designing the interior of Swanney's squalid flat, a task that recalled *Shallow Grave*. 'In *Shallow Grave* the flat was almost like a fourth character,' she said. 'It did things to the people who lived in it, whereas in *Trainspotting* the sets are much more of a background and the characters almost camouflage themselves against them. At times the sets are reflective of the inner state of the characters. An obvious example is Tommy's flat. When he's happy and has a girlfriend, the place is very neat and tidy and quite pleasant, then as he gets hooked on drugs the walls develop an almost veiny feel and the place starts to fall to pieces – like his body.'

During the process of scouting locations in both Glasgow and Edinburgh, where a couple of days' location shooting was to take place, Andrew Macdonald fell ill, leaving the bulk of the task to Danny Boyle. Additionally, for the final sequences of the film, locations in London had to be secured. Three weeks were spent filming the studio scenes in a disused factory, before the location shooting began. The principal photography took seven weeks in total to complete – five days more than the team had on *Shallow Grave*.

As on *Shallow Grave* the trio behind the film took advantage of the opportunity to appear before the camera. Despite his poor opinion of his own acting efforts in *Shallow Grave*, John Hodge turned up in uniform as a security guard in the film's opening sequence, while Andrew Macdonald shakily played the part of half of a flat-hunting couple shown round a property by Renton when he's hiding out in London. Even author Irvine Welsh dubiously got into the act, playing a cameo as Renton's drug dealer Mother Superior – so named for the length of his habit.

For Boyle the rehearsal period was as crucial as it had been on *Shallow Grave*. '*Trainspotting* deals with a group of very close friends,' he noted, 'so it was important that these actors, most of whom had never met each other before, got to know each other and felt comfortable.' As well as rehearsing the script, the cast watched a series of movies selected by Boyle which he hoped would give them an idea of the kind of approach he wanted to take. Among them were *A Clockwork Orange*, *The Hustler*, *GoodFellas*, *The Exorcist* and Kathryn Bigelow's little-known and under-appreciated vampire western *Near Dark*.

'Danny had a really clear idea of how he wanted the film to look,' according to Ewan. 'He had a scrapbook filled with photos and images which he showed us, so that right from the word go you have a good idea of what quality, texture, he wants the film to have and how he's going to shoot it: lots of very low and very high angles, lots of feet and leg shots. In a certain sense, he knows exactly what he wants, but that doesn't mean you have to recreate his imaginings of a scene, he'll let you find it yourself. Working with Danny, he makes you feel almost as though the film's already been made and we just have to find it.'

There were also lessons for the cast in the mechanics and rituals of drug-taking so that they would appear as convincing as possible. The advice and help from the Calton Athletic rehab centre was crucial. 'It was grim,' Ewan said of listening to the harrowing stories told by the recovering addicts. 'I remember these two lads being brought there by their mother and listening to all the stories. The guilt of addicts, about how they treated their mothers, comes up again and again.'

It wasn't all doom and gloom, though, as the relationship between McGregor, the rest of the cast and the recovered addicts was mostly positive. 'We played football with them a lot during rehearsals and throughout filming and they cuffed us every time,' Ewan admitted wryly. 'You couldn't believe they were recovering addicts because they were running circles round us and we were all coughing up our last twenty cigarettes.'

Ewan also turned to drug addicts from Leith for advice on the etiquette of the drug underworld. 'We asked them about the scene where we get put in a taxi by our dealer,' said the actor. 'They all said that would never ever happen. They might put you in a lift and send you down to the ground floor, but that would be it. People OD all over the place, it's just part of the package.' But despite the advice, Macdonald and Boyle decided the scene was dramatically correct and should stay. They credited editor Masahiro Hirakubo for cutting the scene to Lou Reed's 'Perfect Day' – which was to cost the production a huge sum in licensing fees, long before the BBC adopted it as an anthem for public service broadcasting.

. . . I couldn't have played Renton feeling like that.'

Even with all the preparation, Ewan found himself still unprepared for some of the more dramatic real-life action. 'There's a thing about needles, and I think it's why people are so shocked about heroin addicts. There was this scene where, after I OD, the nurse gives me an injection of anti-opiates to bring me back. And they gave me a real injection of saline! I was lying there and I couldn't react to the needle going in, because I was supposed to be in a state of unconsciousness. But I was kind of ready to have a needle in my arm then . . . I'd been pretending to do it for weeks and I was kind of like, "Go on, then, go on. Stick it in my arm." Which is quite peculiar . . .'

Perhaps the most notorious scene of the film is where Renton discovers the worst public toilet in the whole of Scotland, a scene etched indelibly on the memory of anyone who has seen the film – and on the memory of the unfortunate actor. 'Oh God yes, all the toilet stuff was very bleak. It's true to say I felt a bit sick that day. That day was like, "Please can I get off this set, it's disgusting." It was horrible.'

Ewan found playing Renton to be more mentally draining than physically tiring – after all, the character does spend a fair proportion of the movie on his back. There were some scenes in particular that drew from him his finest abilities. 'There's a scene where we discover a dead baby, and that's a very demanding, horrible scene – but then that's quite a challenge and a kick as well, because you're acting it. It's demanding and rewarding. Sometimes it's more demanding sitting listening to other people have a chat about a biscuit, or something, because you don't know what you're supposed to be doing. If you find a dead baby it's actually very clear what you're supposed to be doing, I think . . .'

For Danny Boyle it was the lack of showiness in the performance that made the character of Mark Renton work, especially when he's surrounded by such over-the-top characters as Begbie and 'actorly' turns like Ewen Bremner and Johnny Lee Miller. 'There's a lot of difference between not doing anything and doing nothing,' Boyle claimed. 'Renton is very modern, he doesn't show

Above: Four junkies out on the Scottish Highlands, Renton (Ewan), Sick Boy (Jonny Lee Miller), Tommy (Kevin McKidd) and Spud (Ewen Bremner).
Below: Renton with the menacing Begbie (Robert Carlyle) and Spud (Ewen Bremner).

'Mark Renton is the book's strongest voice. The other characters were structured around him.'

much emotion, he becomes what you want him to be. Ewan has that thing that Caine or Connery had. He's dependable, friendly, accessible, even though he's playing a very weak character. He lets the film happen around him.'

Editing, which began in July 1995, took eight weeks. Hirakubo found it a difficult film to edit 'because it doesn't have a proper narrative flow, which means that one scene won't necessarily relate to the next. Also, it has a lot of music scenes and voice-overs, all of which have to come together. I ended up working twelve-hour days on it.'

While Boyle and Hirakubo toiled away in the editing suite, Macdonald turned his attention to marketing, creating a teaser trailer and liaising with a publicity firm over poster ideas. A few hours after the final scene had been shot, the key cast members were in a Bayswater photographic studio for a series of shots that would ultimately end up on an iconic poster.

> **Boyle claimed: 'Ewan has that thing that Caine or Connery had. He's dependable, friendly, accessible, even though he's playing a very weak character. He lets the film happen around him.'**

At this stage, Ewan became aware that, because of the touchy subject matter of the film, gaining an 18 certificate for release in the UK might be difficult without cutting key scenes. 'It'd be such a shame to start taking bits out of it and start fucking about with it,' he said at the time. 'I hope that doesn't happen with a passion, because I'd like people to see the film that Danny and Andrew put together.'

However in November 1995, as the teaser trailer was screening in cinemas, Britain's film censors, the British Board of Film Classification, passed the movie as an 18 certificate with no cuts. While the film had cost only £1.5 million to make, the marketing budget escalated to around £800,000, compared to the more normal spend of about £200,000 for a UK release. Polygram, who had bought the cinema distribution rights, were determined to make *Trainspotting* into an 'event movie'.

The world premiere took place in Scotland on 16 February 1996, raising funds for Calton Athletic Rehabilitation Centre. The film was screened simultaneously in Edinburgh where tickets sold out in 30 minutes, and Glasgow where they went in 90 minutes. Macdonald, Hodge and Boyle appeared to introduce the movie in Edinburgh, then rapidly headed to Glasgow in time to appear for the film's conclusion and after-show party. Despite his character displaying a huge slice of Scottish self-hatred in the film, Ewan was happy to see it debuting in his native land. Disagreeing with Renton's view of being Scottish, McGregor wouldn't want to be any other way. 'I'm fiercely proud to be Scottish. I don't live there anymore. I chose to live in London, and I love it there. But I'm Scottish through and through. It's a great place, a beautiful land and a beautiful people.'

Like *Shallow Grave* before it, *Trainspotting* opens at breakneck pace as Renton and the gang run down Edinburgh's Princes Street with store security (including John Hodge) in pursuit after a shoplifting spree goes wrong. To McGregor's rhythmic voice-over of the now famous 'choose life' speech, the main characters are introduced and the world of the heroin addict is set up. Just like *Shallow Grave*, the film deepens and gets darker as it progresses; the light-hearted celebration of anarchy at the beginning gives way to a sharper, more despondent tone as the drugs start to have a debilitating effect on the group of friends. Doom and disaster loom among the humorous escapades. Eventually escape is the only route left to Renton, and the final part of the plot revolves around the whereabouts of a stash of ill-gotten cash – just as in *Shallow Grave*. (The team would shamelessly repeat this device for a third time in *A Life Less Ordinary*.) Despite the complaints about *Trainspotting* promoting heroin use, the finished film turns out to be loaded with warnings about the dangers of addiction.

Trainspotting was an instant hit, despite comment from newspapers like the *Daily Mail* that it was 'a disgusting little film', and veteran film critic Alexander Walker in the *Evening Standard* suggesting that it 'makes one puke'. Clearly, these critics were not the audience *Trainspotting* was aiming for, and the film did very well by attracting the young audience whose lives the film was closer to. Within four weeks of the 23 February release in Britain the film had taken £5.4 million, more than *Shallow Grave* had made over its entire release. After it hit screens in America in 1996, *Trainspotting* would take $70 million worldwide, making it one of the most profitable films of the year, according to *Variety*.

In reviewing the film when it was screened out of competition – just like *Shallow Grave* – at the Cannes Film Festival in May 1995, *Variety* complained about a different aspect which might cause it problems in America. *Trainspotting* featured 'in-your-face-realism, cinematic fantasy and four letter dialogue which sets new standards in screen profanity'. But not just the four-letter dialogue, *all* the dialogue in *Trainspotting* was to prove problematic for an American audience, delivered as it was in a variety of thick Scottish accents. The film ended up being dubbed or subtitled for foreign release, even in English-speaking territories.

The furore surrounding *Trainspotting* and the fact he became a pin-up surprised no one more than Ewan himself. Sought after for press and magazine interviews, he suddenly found himself regarded as a 'hot' actor and the subject of countless 'sexiest man alive' polls. 'It's like asking do you think of yourself as a sexy person,' he said in reaction to the acclaim suddenly heaped upon him. 'There is no answer to these questions. I don't waste my time imagining myself as these things. They are things people can think of you as. It is very difficult when people write about you. I only read things and am relieved when people don't slag you off or go, "fuck off" – because they have.'

Despite Ewan's modesty, *Trainspotting* director Danny Boyle saw a great future for his star. 'Every so often we produce an actor here like Gary Oldman or Daniel Day-Lewis, someone who's got the ability to impregnate America on America's own terms. It would not surprise me if Ewan were to become the next big thing. He lets the film happen to him and he's very crafty.'

A few months into their relationship, Ewan and Eve decided to get married. Plans were laid, but of course McGregor's acting commitments got in the way of setting a date. It was not until July 1995 that the marriage took place. They borrowed a house from Ewan's agent Jonathan Altaras with a huge garden and a pool in the Dordogne village of Festalemps in France, 'so we could do it our way'. Over the week various family members and around 60 friends arrived, stayed a few days and then left, with the wedding ceremony in the middle.

The wedding was solemnised in the local town hall and was conducted by a farmer, who as a town official conducted the ceremony wearing a coloured sash. Ewan had come straight to France soon after wrapping shooting on *Trainspotting*, so he wasn't looking his best for the wedding photos. His hair hadn't had time to grow very much and his weight certainly hadn't returned to its normal level. Eve may have been blooming, but Ewan was not a particularly pretty picture.

Along with other members of the extended McGregor family, Jim and Carol had flown out to France to attend their son's wedding. According to Jim, he'd never seen his son so nervous as when he stood up to deliver his speech, even though he professionally delivers speeches to camera.

Despite picking up some French from Eve, McGregor claims not to have fully understood the ceremony. 'All I said was "Oui" and I'm not sure I said that at the right time. But after the ceremony, we gave a party that lasted a week. We all cooked for each other at night,' he recalled, 'and drank fine wines in the garden. It felt like absolutely what we wanted to do. That's very unusual, when you have a dream, to actually see it totally realised, which our marriage was. It was perfect.'

Above: Ewan with the Trainspotting *team at the Cannes Film Festival 1996; Andrew McDonald, Irvine Welsh, Danny Boyle, Ewan and John Hodge.*
Right: Ewan and his wife Eve together at the Cannes Film Festival 1996.

CHAPTER 6
THE LONG WAY AROUND

FROM PLAYING THE STRUNG-OUT, DESPERATE RENTON in *Trainspotting* to tackling the role of debonair charming cad Frank Churchill in Jane Austen's *Emma* was something of a leap of the imagination, even for an actor as seemingly versatile as Ewan McGregor. It was perhaps to prove a jump too far, as neither Ewan nor the critics were enamoured of his performance. The lure for Ewan – as always – was the screenplay. 'I've read a lot of period adaptations and most of them bore me to death in script form,' he admitted. 'This one managed to get very witty dialogue; I thought it had a really good pace to it.'

There was to be no let-up. He'd gone straight from *Trainspotting* to a costume fitting session for *Emma*, then off to France for his wedding. Now he was back in England, preparing to tackle his first period role since the television drama *Scarlet and Black*.

'On the first day of shooting, I was riding horses and wearing a top hat, tails and gloves. And I realised that three weeks before, I'd been lying on a floor in Scotland with a skinned head and needles and syringes all around. I wondered what I was doing. Yet I enjoyed it.'

It may have seemed like an unusual move for the American writer-director of *Emma*, Douglas McGrath, to cast Ewan in the role of Frank Churchill when the actor was best known for his contemporary, cynical roles in *Shallow Grave* and *Trainspotting*. McGrath, though, was looking back to *Scarlet and Black* in his belief that he'd found the right man for the role. He wanted to be faithful to the material, yet produce a bright, hopefully funny film using contemporary acting talent.

'A kind of frightfully charming character' is how Ewan described his role. 'Everyone will hate him, because he's just so bloody charming, which is really annoying.'

To date, Ewan had not played a leading role as such. He'd been canny enough instead to appear as a key player in several ensemble casts, which had all relied on the performances of a group of actors rather than focusing on one, although Ewan had always managed to come out of each film as the one audiences remembered. It was a good way of developing his craft without having to make or break the film – but somehow, Ewan always managed to find himself being singled out.

'Frank Churchill is the life and soul of the party. Sickeningly so,' was how he described his scene-stealing role in *Emma*. 'It's all "Ha, ha, ha, Frank's here, now the fun will start."'

There's a reason for the character's over-the-top heartiness. He's secretly engaged to Jane Fairfax (Polly Walker) and he knows only too well that the rich aunt in London who has adopted him will never approve the match. When he makes one of his periodic visits to Highbury, the family home, to see his father (James Cosmo), he makes a big thing of playing the field by flirting with everything in skirts. 'The trick doesn't work, of course; the town's too small,' Ewan noted. 'But it does serve a purpose, if only as a new topic of gossip for those endless dinner parties.'

With his approach to films as a jobbing actor, Ewan simply saw *Emma* as another piece of work to be tackled as professionally as possible. 'I just enjoy being in the film in question, whether the role is disreputable or dead posh,' he said. 'I love acting. I loved being the caddish Frank Churchill in *Emma*, except the wig itched a lot. I loved being in *Trainspotting* and having to dive into the filthiest toilet in Scotland. I loved being Jerome, lying around with no clothes on while a beautiful woman wrote all over me in Peter Greenaway's *The Pillow Book*. I also enjoyed *Brassed Off*, playing Andy, a miner who plays the tenor horn in the colliery brass band.'

He didn't feel the kind of research he'd done for *Trainspotting* was needed for his new role. 'I don't have to live a character,' he said. 'I think there's almost an element there, subconsciously. For example, I think I was slightly more aggressive than I normally am when I was playing Renton. When I was playing Alex in *Shallow Grave*, I was quite rude to some people, though only to people who deserved it. When you're concentrating on certain aspects of someone else's personality, it brings your attention to those aspects in your own character.'

Left: The lure for Ewan to play Frank Churchill in Emma *was the screenplay.*
Above and below: McGregor's Andy gets to woo Tara Fitzgerald's Gloria as they play in the local pit band in Brassed Off.

Struck by the book when he first read it two years after graduating from Princeton, playwright McGrath was surprised no one had made a film version of the novel. 'If you want to turn a classic into a film you can't do better than Austen. The material adapts naturally. The stories advance through discussion and there's not much interior monologue.' It was the kind of screenwriting project John Hodge might have preferred to the intricacies of *Trainspotting*.

'A lot of writers adapting a book they know is a classic become ponderous and reverential,' McGrath pointed out, insisting that *Emma* needed a different approach. 'Austen is breezy, romantic and fun. When I first read *Emma*, it seemed so light, I was surprised that the book didn't float out of my hands.'

'I was riding horses and wearing a top hat. And I realised that three weeks before, I'd been lying on a floor in Scotland with a skinned head and needles and syringes all around. I wondered what I was doing. Yet I enjoyed it.'

Emma is a misguided match-maker, who in trying and failing to match her friend Harriet up with various seemingly eligible bachelors (Jeremy Northam as Knightley, Ewan as Churchill, Alan Cumming as young vicar Mr Elton and Edward Woodall as local farmer Mr Martin) singularly fails to see the romances right before her eyes, both for herself and Harriet.

Douglas McGrath seemed happy to take risks all around in his casting of the movie – from picking American actress Gwyneth Paltrow (best known then for featuring in *Seven* and being Brad Pitt's girlfriend) to play the quintessential English Emma to Australian Toni Collette (from comedy *Muriel's Wedding*) as Emma's trusting friend Harriet Smith. 'I was quite happy to change a few preconceived ideas,' he said of his approach to Jane Austen's 1816 novel. As McGrath was the co-writer, with Woody Allen, of *Bullets Over Broadway* (1994), this version of *Emma* promised to be unique.

'The book, for example, is set in Surrey and many people believe Cobham was the model for Highbury. Our production designer convinced me that Dorset, with its fantastic countryside and Georgian architecture, was where we should be,' said McGrath. 'It meant completely changing many scenes I'd visualised, sitting at my desk in New York.'

'His loose approach to the material allowed for locations to influence the way some scenes were shot. According to production designer Michael Howells, McGrath 'reworked the scene where Emma first meets Frank and set it by the ford at Morton, instead of in the wood he originally had in mind.' The village of Evershot, where much of the location filming took place, was redressed extensively to place it in period, while several stately homes, including Stafford House and Mapperton, were also used for authenticity.

The production was a speedy one – as most of McGregor's films seem to have been. After only 41 days, principal shooting had been wrapped. McGrath was determined to capture some of the light breeziness of the subject matter in the way he made the film. 'It was a way of injecting pace into our approach,' he confirmed. 'I wrote it to play fast. There are occasions when Emma starts a sentence at the end of a scene, then we cut and she finishes the sentence at the start of another scene in new clothes in a different place. That's a comic effect, too.'

The finished film is a delightful piece of work, making Austen accessible to modern audiences through the use of young star names in the key roles and highlighting the gossip and meddling which Emma indulges in. Of the film's performances, though, only Gwyneth Paltrow comes out well, with her impeccable English accent (which also featured in *Sliding Doors*) proving a big surprise. Alongside Jeremy Northam and Alan Cumming, Ewan was having to compete quite hard for top prize in the hammy acting stakes.

'I never read the novel – it really bored me to death – and I wasn't really committed to it,' he admitted of what he considered to be his poor performance as Frank Churchill, a pantomime turn he disparagingly called 'ha-ha-ha curly wig acting'. 'I don't think I was very good in it – my performance is fucking dreadful. The only time I've done work I thought was no good was when I didn't go with my gut instincts. There are lessons to be learned.'

He was sure that if his performance was as off as he came to believe during shooting that McGrath would point it out. He was especially thrown by the daft wig he had to wear. 'It's a funny thing, when you're looking in the mirror and you think, they must know . . .?,' the actor admitted. 'But they never said "The hair looks fucking ridiculous." Still, I can't blame the hair – I was just particularly awful.'

Reviewers seemed to agree. Todd McCarthy, writing in *Variety*, complained the film was 'filled out with peripheral characters', prime among them being 'dashing stranger Frank Churchill'. Others thought that McGregor was simply unsuited to period roles. Writing in the *Sunday Telegraph*, Chris Peachment noted that he was 'rather too modern in idiom', while Philip French in the *Observer* wrote: 'less satisfactory is the role of Frank Churchill (McGregor), whose charm and cruelty are mentioned, but not dramatised'.

Adam Mars-Jones in the *Independent* was more positive and thought there was 'nothing in Ewan McGregor's past life on screen that would suggest his suitability for playing Frank Churchill, but the discrepancy of his acting style pays a dividend. It becomes part of the character's dangerous charm that he enters a conspiracy with the person he's talking to, as if they alone know what is real and what is not.'

In the States *Emma* was a big critical hit. Roger Ebert of the *Chicago Sun-Times* noted: 'Gwyneth Paltrow sparkles in the title role. There is a dashing young bachelor in the neighbourhood named Frank Churchill (Ewan McGregor) who seems cast as her beau, he rescues her when her carriage gets mired in the river.' The *San Francisco Chronicle* called *Emma* 'lightweight but likable . . . McGrath has accepted a likable Hollywood comedy from Austen's book, and here and there some of the social satire squeaks through.'

Another bugbear McGregor had with *Emma* was having to return to the English accent he'd adopted for his TV work in *Lipstick on Your Collar* and *Scarlet and Black*, after becoming comfortable using his own accent in *Shallow Grave* and *Trainspotting*. 'We were forced into doing this very clipped, very proper English accent, so as a result, I wasn't really talking to anyone, I was just trying to sound right. But it's alright – it's alright to do a bad one, you just move on.'

Whatever he felt afterwards, *Emma* had been an enjoyable project to work on, enough for Ewan not to rule out future 'curly wig' roles entirely. 'All actors like dressing up, regardless of what they might say. It's fun, all that stuff, so it's different. There were great people on it – I worked with Toni Collette, she's brilliant, so funny and such a nice person. Gwyneth was there, and Jamie Cosmo, who played my dad in *Trainspotting*, played my dad in *Emma* as well!'

The bad reviews of his performance seemed to do the film no harm, especially in America, where *Emma* took $22 million, compared with *Trainspotting*'s $16 million.

Off screen there were consolations. Shortly after their marriage, Eve told him she was pregnant. Although only 24, McGregor was delighted to be having a child – although he knew it was going to be tough to cope with both his developing family life and his growing star status.

He was not interested in taking the Hollywood route to stardom, so at least he knew he'd probably be able to stay in London. The big question on his mind was whether he'd still be able to secure the kind of roles he wanted in both British and American movies working from a London base and by bringing his family along on location with him – which is what he had decided he would like to do.

'The only time I've done work I thought was no good was when I didn't go with my gut instincts. There are lessons to be learned . . .'

'I met an actress in Los Angeles,' McGregor said, 'who asked me "How long have you been in Los Angeles?" I said, "Well, actually, I live in London." She said: "How does that work?" I mean, how does that work! She couldn't imagine that anyone could make movies outside of Los Angeles.'

For McGregor, staying out of Los Angeles became an end in itself. He was out to prove several seemingly impossible things – that it was possible to have a film career without relocating to America, that it was possible to do that and have a happy family life, and that it was possible to be a father and husband, as well as a movie star at only 24 years of age. So far, he'd succeeded on all three counts.

'There are too many wrecked marriages in this business for mine to be one, and if anyone doesn't like that, I won't make the film. . .

. . . It's important - I don't want to miss my daughter growing up because of a film.'

For Ewan, the low-budget British political and social drama *Brassed Off* was a much better fit with his established cinematic persona. It was his hope that people who had a dim view of his *Emma* performance would take the time to see him in *Brassed Off*. 'I play closer to the real me than I've done before,' he said.

His part in the film is Andy, a young coal miner who plays tenor horn in a miners' band which reaches the national competition finals, just as their coal mine faces closure. 'Andy is a bit dour and very pessimistic about the future of the coal industry, because that future is his future. He's in a desperate situation and is genuinely trying to hold on to the final threads of optimism, but it's an uphill struggle. It's based on a true story and it's a really brilliantly political piece of film-making,' he claimed. 'The politics are so strong and the music is so emotional. I liked the politics of it. It was saying something for all those poor guys who worked in mines.'

'The studio system in LA is about money. They just make me cold and they turn out such awful crap.'

The politics of the piece were clear in Mark Herman's script, which had been Ewan's first contact with the movie. 'Sometimes, you get a script and you think – well, there's something here and I like it, but it'll take a lot of work from the actors to get it kick-started. Then there are the "special" scripts. They're totally unlike the ones where things might come alive. They are the one's you read where you think, "Bloody hell, that's got a bit of zip to it," and that was most definitely the case with *Brassed Off*. From the moment I read it, I knew I had to be part of the project.'

For writer-director Mark Herman the political content of *Brassed Off* was the entire point. Herman, along with producer Steve Abbot, had supported the 1984 miners' strike in Britain. 'I had lots of ideas about the issues I wanted to tackle,' he said, 'but no peg to hang it on.'

A newspaper article about a Northern pit village with a strong tradition of making music caught Herman's attention. The piece mentioned the local brass band, celebrated for the quality of their playing. He was struck by the fact that such a musical endeavour could spring up among the hardships facing those still in coal mining. There was also a strong dramatic angle to the tale. 'They were going to have to pack it all in,' Herman recalled, 'because they simply didn't have the money to carry on.' He had found his hook, and soon he had a script.

Now came the casting process, and for Herman, Ewan was ideal for the role: 'He's very restrained. He hardly moves, but you watch him all the time. He has amazing eyes – you can tell so much through the eyes. Isn't that what makes a movie star?'

Brassed Off was another ensemble film, rather than a star vehicle. Apart from the drama of the band's attempts to get to the Albert Hall, the main plot was the father-son relationship between Pete Postlethwaite's Danny and his suicidal and debt-ridden son Phil (Stephen Tompkinson).

McGregor had the romantic sub-plot, getting to woo Tara Fitzgerald's Gloria, who joins the band as flugelhorn player and – unknown to the others – works for the management at the pit. 'The only sunshine in Andy's life is when this lass, Gloria, joins the local pit band. Suddenly things begin to perk up. Since Gloria is played by Tara Fitzgerald, I see what he means,' Ewan noted. In fact he was good friends with Fitzgerald before *Brassed Off* brought them together on screen.

Playing tenor horn was not a problem as Ewan had played French horn in his youth. 'It was very similar, so I was able to tootle along with the tunes, which was quite acceptable … but you certainly don't hear me playing – I left that to the professionals. Well, I picked it up, but I couldn't play nearly as well as the experts there played. I could hold a tune, almost. All the brass band – apart from the actors – are the real Grimethorpe Colliery Band, and the story is really based on their story. Brass band music isn't something that's hugely popular with my generation, but when they started up, it was incredible sitting amongst all that passionate knowledge. And they're a good bunch of lads, too.'

Brassed Off was shot on location in Grimethorpe, Halifax, Doncaster and the surrounding villages of South Yorkshire. From Frank Churchill to Andy was another quick change for Ewan.

During breaks while filming *Emma*, he had locked himself away in his trailer to work on learning the script for *Brassed Off* and to listen to tapes of Yorkshire accents in order to develop his own. Ewan arrived on the set word-perfect and accent intact, ready to turn in one of his most natural performances, certainly one that was a million miles away from *Emma*.

The reviewers were much more enthusiastic about this low-budget, charming and politically committed film. In the *Evening Standard*, Alexander Walker wrote that 'McGregor and Fitzgerald keep their mutual attraction on hold until they can make rousing music of a strictly asexual kind together.' Quentin Curtis, in the *Daily Telegraph*, called McGregor 'relaxed but riveting' in the role, while in the *Village Voice*, Amy Taubin claimed that 'McGregor is that rare thing – an unabashedly romantic actor.' In *Time Out*, critic Anne Billson found that 'Ewan McGregor looks more at ease in jeans than he ever did in Jane Austen's breeches.'

Unlike *Trainspotting* and *Emma*, *Brassed Off* did little in the United States. It was hardly given the opportunity. Pete Postlethwaite starred in Steven Spielberg's *The Lost World: Jurassic Park* as well as *Brassed Off*, both of which opened at the same time in America. The dinosaur sequel had 3281 screens nationwide, while McGregor's trumpet-blowing was only available on a total of twelve. Nevertheless, *Brassed Off* managed to gross $2.5 million in the US to add to the £2.8 million taken in the UK.

As a prospective father at the age of only 24, McGregor was nervous, confessing to one movie magazine that he was 'falling to bits' due to the waiting. Finally, in February 1996, the big day arrived. He and Eve had an early start, as her contractions began in the middle of the night. 'I'd practised the route to the hospital millions of times but I still managed to take the wrong turning when it actually happened,' he admitted. 'Thank God it was four in the morning. It was a long, complicated labour. All you can see is the person you love in the most awful pain. Your're worrying about the baby being alright and your wife being alright, and it's terrifying.' It was a short trip from their flat on the edge of London's Regent's Park to the hospital, where McGregor's worries were to prove well-founded. Clara Mathilde McGregor, as his daughter was to be called, had a somewhat traumatic birth, with Eve having to undergo a Caesarean section, after a 24-hour labour.

The experience was more fraught for Ewan than any acting challenge ever could be. 'I wasn't prepared to be that frightened,' he remembered. 'I imagined you had to be this rock for your wife and I just got more and more frightened the longer it went on, that something was going to go wrong. In the end she had the Caesarean section and I had to go in there and all I was thinking was, "Oh no, I'm not big enough for this, not quite sure if I can handle this one."'

After the birth, McGregor spent the night at home alone whilst his wife and newly born daughter remained under observation in the hospital. 'I arrived home in a daze and phoned a lot of people,' he remembered. 'I was crying down the phone to my parents at 6.30a.m.'

As he tried to sleep, he knew that his life had changed in a way more dramatic than any amount of fame and fortune through the movies could bring about. 'I dunno, you feel like a completely different person. You've gone through the biggest emotional experience of your life, and this is what you've left behind. This is "before" and you're already in the "after". You can never go back.'

Ewan realised that his regular alcohol binges would have to become something of the past, though he knew he'd miss nights out with his mates. 'I'll be at home, with the nappies. Maybe I've made a terrible mistake!' he joked, before admitting that at heart he's more suited to family life than a life of debauchery. 'I dunno. All I know is it's so good to have them with me, it's so good for me, I'm so much happier than I used to be. I've got these people to keep me in check.'

It was also clear that although the Regent's Park flat had just about coped with Eve moving her stuff in, there was no way that the McGregor family of three could stay there. Once Eve and Clara were out of the hospital, Ewan had to give some thought to relocating. The result was the purchase of a townhouse near St John's Wood and Belsize Park in London. The cost of the new home, believed to be in the region of £1.25 million, was something Ewan refused to confirm when journalists asked, seemingly embarrassed at being able to spend that amount of money. He was beginning to discover the material rewards of his workaholic nature and growing star status.

'I don't care enough about breaking in to America to give a shit about it. Where I am now, there can't be a better place for an actor to be.'

'It's pretty common knowledge that I spend half my free time drinking and the other half dealing with my hangovers, it's not a life I recommend, but it's mine.'

Above: Ewan with co-star Patricia Arquette in the ill-fated Nightwatch.

Below: Besotted by the beautiful Thea (Carmen Chaplin) in The Serpent's Kiss.

However, buying the house wasn't enough. Ewan and Eve decided to employ architects and designers to restructure the property overall so that it would suit their needs better. It was more flexing of financial muscle in the service of his new family.

Eschewing the glamour of stardom, Ewan McGregor quickly became devoted to his new domestic life. He enjoyed spending time with Clara and Eve, whether it was doing up the new house or taking a walk in the park. He'd get away on his own or with some friends to play golf if he felt the need to escape the domestic pressures. Another way of spending time off from the family was to go for a ride on his motorbike – the interest he'd inherited from Marie Pairis. 'I've got an old '74 Motoguzzi,' he revealed. 'It's nice, a bit heavy for town, but it's a good bike. I saw a really nice Harley the other day, a sweet one. I'm thinking of taking it home, but I don't know if it'll be suitable for London. It would be good to go around Europe on.'

It was, though, to be a while before the McGregor family would get a chance to spend some time together away from a film set, as Ewan was about to jet off to America to make his first real Hollywood film – an ambition he'd harboured since childhood.

'I'm just into making quality stuff if I can, with interesting people and good scripts. But it's very important that it's about something and that it says something.'

The first thought that entered Ewan's head on seeing Los Angeles was, 'It looks like the world's biggest caravan park. It's the place to go when you're making a film, fine, but you'd lose all your critical faculties if you stayed. It's valium-haze LA.'

Los Angeles – more specifically, Hollywood – had been beckoning since *Shallow Grave* had made such a big impact. He'd been courted by studios and agents – along with Hodge, Macdonald and Boyle – at the time, but had firmly resisted all offers. However, after *Trainspotting* the clamour from USA for Ewan to make a movie there was becoming too much to ignore.

If he were to relocate to America, Ewan would simply be following in a long line of footsteps, from Gary Oldman to Tim Roth to Kenneth Brannagh and Hugh Grant. America, after all, was where the movie industry was based. However, although making it big in Hollywood might have been a childhood fantasy when he'd absorbed all those black and white melodramas, now that he was an adult, Ewan had come to realise that he didn't need America to make it as a successful film actor, after all. 'I had people in LA tell me, "You've got to understand – you've got to do one [film] for yourself and then two for the industry." What the fuck does that mean? I'm not doing it for the money, I'm doing it because I can't read a good script and say no.'

Yet despite his determination to play the acting game his way, it does seem likely that *Nightwatch* came about because Ewan finally accepted the advice of his agents to try his hand at a commercial American movie – albeit a remake of a European film with the original director at the helm. It was that element of the plan that may have given Ewan the reason to go ahead.

The new version of *Nightwatch*, like the original Danish thriller *Nattevagten*, was directed by Ole Borendal. 'I wonder if he just directed the same film again? I don't know,' mused McGregor. 'He's got a great director of photography, who's Danish and also worked on the first version. The sets were very good and it has a very good cast – Nick Nolte, Patricia Arquette and Josh Brolin.'

In fact, with a new screenplay by Steven Soderbergh, the $10 million *Nightwatch* wasn't just the same film again, but a re-interpretation. The suspense thriller told the story of young law student Martin Belos (McGregor) who takes a part-time job as a lone hospital night watchman just as a serial killer has begun to terrorise the city. Investigating the case is Inspector Cray (Nolte). Even more frightening than the murders are the clues, which keep leading back to Belos. As the police close in, this seemingly innocent man becomes a prime suspect. To solve the crime, he has to stay wide awake on the job in the hope of catching the real culprit.

The film-making process in Hollywood was a real eye-opener for Ewan, used to working in the cash-strapped though creative British film industry where every film was a make-or-break project and every penny counted. 'The technicians wore bigger tool belts,' he said of *Nightwatch*. 'I noticed lots and lots of tool belts, like holsters for drills and stuff. It's quite slick, because they're working all the time.'

Despite Ewan's interest in the process of making the film, it was clear that production company Miramax were not terribly keen on the completed movie. Shelved immediately after completion, *Nightwatch* wasn't finally released in the States until spring 1998. During the long wait for the film to appear, Ewan was often asked about it. 'I saw a cut of it about a year ago. It was perfectly fine and could have gone out then,' he said just before the film finally debuted. 'I don't know why they haven't put it out. I think they're waiting for one of my really good movies to come out and they'll release that after it.'

Entertainment Weekly, however, was scathing about the film: '*Nightwatch* is meant to be a psychological thriller but is just plain sickening. Why decent actors like McGregor and Nolte signed on is a puzzlement. Bottom Line: A bloody mess.' The best critic Roger Ebert of the *Chicago Sun-Times* could find to say about it was that *Nightwatch* was 'a visually effective and often scary film to watch, but the story is so leaky that we finally just give up'. The *San Francisco Chronicle* felt McGregor was 'handsome yet slightly seedy' and 'McGregor's American accent wobbles in and out, but it's amusing to watch the British struggle with that for a change.'

One of the worries the producers of the film had after they'd wrapped was that Ewan's character was perhaps a bit too passive to be a true American celluloid hero. They wanted him to return to do a series of action-oriented re-shoots to pep the film up a bit. He refused.

'They all talk about budgets and meetings,' he said of the non-creative business end of the Hollywood film-making machine. 'The last thing anybody seems to be worried about is the movie. A-lists and B-lists of actors – fuck, that's disgusting. "We got a B-lister and a couple of Cs, now we need a couple of As . . ." No you don't – you need the right person for the part. The way they just talk business, it has got nothing to do with making good films. The studio system in LA is about money. They just make me cold and they turn out such awful crap.'

After it's American release, *Nightwatch* went directly to video in the UK, much to Ewan's annoyance. 'It was a waste of my time,' he said of the movie. 'You don't make films for them to disappear. Mind you, I'm pretty glad it did now, because it didn't turn out the way I hoped.'

Ewan's two months in Los Angeles had not been pleasant. He'd been away from his wife and newborn daughter, didn't enjoy being in America and didn't even get to work much with his co-stars. He only briefly met Patricia Arquette, who played his girlfriend in the film, as their scenes were all shot within the first week of filming. It was a lonely process, and one that made him more determined than before to stay based in Britain, even if he would be making movies in America occasionally: 'I don't care enough about breaking in to America to give a shit about it. Where I am now, there can't be a better place for an actor to be.'

One of the few highlights of his time in Hollywood was Oscar night: 'It was like Christmas! We had a brilliant time, went to all these parties, behaved really badly. Even that night, I thought, it'd be great to be in there, to win one and not feel like they did. To be in and still on the outside.'

Back from America, Ewan was scheduled to join his *Brassed Off* co-star, Pete Postlethwaite, in Ireland to star in *The Serpent's Kiss*, a film he'd committed to make some nine months earlier. Like *Emma*, *The Serpent's Kiss* was a period piece, this time set in Gloucestershire, England, in 1699.

For filming, Ewan, Eve and Clara Mathilde relocated to Sixmilebridge, County Clare in Ireland for the best part of three months so he could concentrate on the two-month shooting schedule of the film. Happily for Ewan, after the night shooting on *Nightwatch*, most of *The Serpent's Kiss* was shot during the day, leaving evenings free for him to spend with Eve and Clara. It was a relaxing time for him, and he found that the filming proceeded remarkably easily.

The Serpent's Kiss is a story of landscape gardening, sexual intrigue and deceit in which Ewan plays the flamboyant Meneer Chrome, a Dutch gardener hired by a pompous, *nouveau riche* factory owner Thomas Smithers (Pete Postlethwaite) to design and build a garden for his bored wife Juliana (Greta Scacchi).

Juliana has little time for her husband, is bored by her isolation in the country and has no interest in horticulture. However, she swiftly develops more than a passing fancy for the earnest, handsome young Dutchman. Though flattered by Juliana's attentions, Chrome is clearly more interested in her daughter Thea (Carmen Chaplin), a wild child who feels ill at ease in formal domestic surroundings.

With the arrival of Fitzmaurice (Richard E. Grant), Juliana's fashionable but impoverished cousin, the plans for the garden seem to grow in scope, ambition and expense. Elaborate hot

The Serpent's Kiss. *Above: Chrome (Ewan) falling under Thea's spell.*
Below: Greta Scacchi as Chrome's manipulative employer Juliana.

Serpent's Kiss Director Philippe Rousselot: 'Ewan is an incredible actor. He looks great and he's perfect for the role. He was the first to be cast.'

houses are constructed. The venture takes on outlandish proportions. As Chrome falls further under Thea's spell, his disenchantment with both the project and Smithers' treatment of his daughter manifests itself. It becomes clear that Fitzmaurice has had a hold over him from the very outset. In an effort to win Juliana, the jealous Fitzmaurice has blackmailed Chrome to bring about Smithers' financial ruin.

But Fitzmaurice's plans are complicated by Juliana's passion for Chrome and by Chrome's falling deeply in love with Thea. With Juliana's assistance, Chrome is compelled to confront his dilemma. Fitzmaurice, however, has other ideas and is quite prepared to kill to achieve his aims.

Ewan stuck with the project whilst international funding was sought, despite being offered several more lucrative roles. The screenplay by Tim Rose Price was, according to McGregor, 'one of the best I've read in a long time and it's beautifully written'.

Producer Robert Jones, whose credits include *The Usual Suspects*, thought that the film was lucky indeed to have Ewan as a leading player. 'Ewan is a joy to work with. He's incredibly focused and a very genuine guy. This film was a long time getting going and he could have walked a hundred times, but he stuck with it despite very heavy pressures. Everybody wants to work with him.'

The film was the first directed by the French cinematographer, Philippe Rousselot, who won an Oscar for *A River Runs Through It* with Brad Pitt. 'Ewan is an incredible actor,' Rousselot said on the set. 'He looks great and he's perfect for the role. He was the first to be cast.' When discussing Ewan's growing star status, Rousselot admitted: 'I have to use clichés, but they're true: fascinating face, the camera loves him, he's very quick, very bright, no fuss. There's no recipe for star quality, but you can't take your eyes off his face.'

The film had its world premiere at Cannes in 1997 but screen time had not been found for it in either the UK or the USA a year later.

'I'm in the optimum, ultimate position for a young actor, to have choice and have work. I understand that and I appreciate that. I feel incredibly lucky and kind of . . . I'm not going to say "blessed", I'm not going to say that. Lucky.'

Such was Ewan's popularity, as 1996 drew to a close, that he was asked to lend his voice to an animated character being used for safety announcements by the Virgin Atlantic airline. It was a nice easy job which took place in a recording studio in London. Taking the work showed that, despite the international stardom and acclaim, McGregor was not above taking on small projects – especially if they involved working with people he considered to be friends.

Commitment to his friends is a strong streak in his character. Actor Jude Law was a close friend long before he became famous himself in films such as *Wilde* and *Gattaca*. Johnny Lee Miller became a friend during the shooting of *Trainspotting*. Both would be involved with Ewan in setting up the film production company Natural Nylon in 1995. Another friend is director Justin Chadwick, who'd directed Ewan in the short *Family Style* for Channel 4 back in 1993.

Because of the connection, Ewan agreed to work with Chadwick again on another short film called *Sleeping with the Fishes,* although even he admitted it could only be a 'weird loyalty thing'. For Britain's most bankable actor in many a long year, committing to a trip to Eastbourne for an ultra-low-budget short film hardly seemed like a good career move.

The twenty-minute short was about 'sex and fish, set in a chip shop'. Some of the shooting took place in the Grand Hotel, Eastbourne, where the cast and crew were also staying. There they would watch the previous day's rushes, an often unintentionally funny experience. Ewan however has never enjoyed watching himself. During a scene of him and leading actress Nadia having semiclothed sex, he partially hid his face in his hands with embarrassment. As his on-screen self began thrusting in Nadia's lap as she balanced precariously on a storeroom counter beside a plate of raw fish fillets, he could take no more. When the scene approached its climax, the plates rattling and falling off the counter, he leapt out of his seat in the makeshift screaming room and shouted: 'Four years of training . . . '

'I get bored with rushes,' he admitted, revealing his perception of a film being complete when he finished it, regardless of post-production work or even audience reception. 'Some directors won't let you see them because they think you'll get all paranoid, but with me it's just boredom: tedious, relentless, take-after-take of yourself, and you just think, "God, I'm so dreary . . . "'

'Dreary' was not a word most would apply to Ewan McGregor in 1996. It had been an amazing year for him: 'Business-wise, I'm in the optimum, ultimate position for a young actor. I've just done a film I've wanted to make for over a year [*The Serpent's Kiss*] and I've got one to go on to with people I've worked with twice before [*A Life Less Ordinary*]. I've got more scripts to read, more choice – it's easier for me to pick and choose. The money side of things is irrelevant. I don't see how you can be in a better position as an actor, to have choice and have work. I understand that and I appreciate that. I feel incredibly lucky and kind of . . . I'm not going to say "blessed", I'm not going to say that. Lucky.'

CHAPTER 7
WORKING WITH ANGELS

BY THE TIME EWAN, NOW 25, started shooting on *A Life Less Ordinary* in Utah late in September 1996, *Trainspotting* fever had reached its height in Britain. Ewan's face had become ubiquitous as posters of the emaciated, water-soaked Renton were stuck onto walls in student halls up and down the land and peered from the pages of countless glossy magazines.

The film had opened in America on 17 July 1996, performing best in urban centres where long queues had formed for the first screenings. This was despite the film coming strongly under attack by anti-drug campaigners for supposedly glamorising drugs and heroin addiction.

Wherever *Trainspotting* opened, the film faced the same accusations, despite the fates that befall the characters. However, film critic of New York's *Newsday* magazine John Anderson took a different view: 'It's challenging in a way that I think we haven't seen since *Pulp Fiction*,' he claimed. 'It makes people uncomfortable, rather than just washing over them like so much Hollywood stuff does.'

As for Ewan himself, his biggest cult success would prove a mixed blessing in the US. 'I've had so much shite out of that film,' he confirmed. 'I got fucking strip searched at Chicago airport. I was doing an episode of *e.r.* [in a guest appearance directed by Quentin Tarantino] and my visa had Warner Brothers on it, and some customs guy asked me about my movies and I said the only ones known in America were *Shallow Grave* and *Trainspotting*. And he says, "Aaaah, *Trainspotting*," and writes something on my form and when I get to the red and green bit they searched me everywhere. Even up the arse. Fucking stupid bastard!'

It was in this atmosphere that Ewan arrived to take the lead role in his third collaboration with the *Shallow Grave* and *Trainspotting* team. Ironically, the location where the filming was to take place, Mormon stronghold Salt Lake City in Utah, had banned *Trainspotting*.

John Hodge had begun working on the screenplay for *A Life Less Ordinary* as far back as 1993, after completing his first draft of *Shallow Grave*. It was a screwball comedy version of the same tale, as a bag of money, shovels and shallow graves were to feature prominently in this new story too. At its heart, though, was a romance formed when a desperate kidnapping goes wrong.

'Although the reality of kidnapping is pretty brutal and murderous, what I wanted to do was use it as a device, a conceit, within which to explore a romantic relationship. The rest of the story grew out of that,' Hodge claimed.

A Life Less Ordinary follows the misadventures of Scottish janitor Robert (Ewan). He's one of life's losers, working for a giant corporation while dreaming of writing a blockbuster novel about the links between JFK and Marilyn Monroe. Fired by the company boss to be replaced by a robot, he uses a chance meeting with the boss's daughter Celine (Cameron Diaz) to kidnap her in the hope of winning his job back – only for Celine to take charge of the situation, leading to a bank robbery to fund their getaway. This might have seemed enough for any one film, but Hodge added another layer of complication by having the pair fated to fall in love, but failing to do so. Out to make things go according to this celestial plan are a pair of less-than-competent angels. The supernatural overtones caught the wave of interest in angels in America, featured in films like John Travolta's *Michael* and the Nicolas Cage – Meg Ryan weepie *City of Angels*.

While the script of *A Life Less Ordinary* progressed, Andrew Macdonald and Danny Boyle were fielding extremely tempting offers from Hollywood. 'A number of projects were very attractive indeed,' recalled Macdonald. 'Particularly the offer to do *Alien 4* [which became *Alien Resurrection*] with Sigourney Weaver and Winona Ryder. The script was great, but after a few meetings, Danny and I realised that it wasn't the kind of film we wanted to do and luckily at that point John was just finishing writing *A Life Less Ordinary*. It seemed a lot more important to do that, and do it our way, rather than do someone else's project.'

For their third film the team had chosen a very different subject matter – it was clear that as a 'romantic comedy', *A Life Less Ordinary* would be nowhere near as dark as either *Shallow Grave* or *Trainspotting*. They set out to make a film in the style of the great American directors of the thirties and forties, Preston Sturges and Billy Wilder, who shunned sentimentality in favour of sharp scripting and great characters. It would be a tall order to live up to for anyone, let alone a film-making team whom critics were just waiting to see fail spectacularly after their double whammy.

Budgeted at $12 million dollars, the now US-set tale of divine intervention was simply too big a project for the team's previous financial backers at Channel 4. They were the first to put up some cash, though, with Macdonald selling the British television screening rights, giving him the funding to scout locations and line up a series of international partners. In the producers' eyes it was important that creative control remain with the writer, producer and director, so Macdonald was determined that they, and not a big American studio, would own the film.

After an abortive trip to North Carolina in search of locations, the team settled on Utah. The fact that North Carolina had been fog-bound when they visited was interpreted by Danny Boyle as a divine sign that this particular state wasn't for them. 'We chose Utah because of the tremendous variety of the landscape,' Macdonald said. 'It has harsh desert, beautiful mountains and a buzzing city, all within a few hours' drive. But Utah is also one of the few states with good film technicians living at home – so that was obviously very important for us.'

'A Life Less Ordinary was everything I could have hoped for and I jumped at the opportunity to do it.'

When it came to casting the central roles, the leading part of young Scotsman Robert, adrift in an alien culture, was easy to fill. Hodge was happy to admit he'd written the role with Ewan in mind, but Andrew Macdonald wasn't going to give their potential lead actor as easy a ride as that.

'They came over to America and watched five scenes that I showed them from *Nightwatch*,' said Ewan of the first discussions he had with his *Trainspotting* pals about starring in *A Life Less Ordinary*. The way he recalls things, it was far from a foregone conclusion that he'd play the role. First off, he understood the character was to be an American, and neither Macdonald nor Boyle were impressed by his attempt at an American accent in *Nightwatch*. 'Then they left it for a couple of days and didn't phone me. I thought, "Fuckin' hell, what the fuck is going on here?" Then they called and said they would like me to do it, that they would just rewrite it as a Scotsman. The American accent didn't wash with them. I was really hurt because I thought I was doing all right!'

As soon as he'd read the screenplay, Ewan knew there was no way he could not be involved in this film. 'I really look forward to reading everything John has written because it's always so unexpected and so funny. *A Life Less Ordinary* was everything I could have hoped for and I jumped at the opportunity to do it. While there are little bits of business you'll recognise from the past two movies we've made together, I wanted to do *A Life Less Ordinary* because it's unashamedly romantic. I love those old thirties and forties romances. They're missing from the cinema today. We're surrounded by too much cynicism. It was a risky project, and there was pressure on all of us after the huge success of *Trainspotting*, but it's good to do stuff you're frightened of.'

As with all his major roles, Ewan is not attracted necessarily by the director, location or pay-packet attached to a project, but simply by the screenplay. 'Reading this script, for instance, wasn't the same experience as reading *Trainspotting*, because *Trainspotting* truly blew me away. In this one, the bones of the storyline are more understood. You meet a girl, you fall in love with her, you lose her and then you get her back. It's not formula, but we understand the bones of the story. So to read it wasn't nearly as mind-blowing; however, the film is so far beyond my image from reading the script the first time. And it's because of their film-making. They're true inspirational film-makers. I have complete trust and faith in them and I know they wouldn't make a bad film. They might make an unsuccessful movie, but I know they wouldn't make a bad one. And the chances of John writing a poor script are pretty much remote anyway.'

The switch from the Scottish setting and concerns of the team's previous films to this huge American adventure was not as much of a leap for Ewan as it was for the other three – he'd had enough experience by now just to approach the film as another in a long succession of diverse roles. He did realise, though, that they were all taking a big risk in trying to take on the

Americans at their own game and on their home turf. 'I think after *Shallow Grave*, *Trainspotting* was a huge risk. I think after *Trainspotting*, *A Life Less Ordinary* was probably a bigger risk. It is a different comedy to the other ones. After *Trainspotting*, the riskiest thing we could do was an American romantic comedy.'

Working on location in America was not going to be a stretch for Ewan, either. At least this time he knew he wouldn't be repeating his *Nightwatch* loneliness and alienation. He'd have his friends around him every day, and his family would be on location with him, too. 'It would probably be smoother in Scotland, we know the score, we all work the same way,' he admitted. 'Whereas an American crew works in a slightly different way . . . It feels weird. There are shots, wide shots in the desert with the bluest sky you have ever seen. And the two characters just walk across the frame . . . '

Since her debut in the Jim Carrey vehicle *The Mask*, Ewan's co-star Cameron Diaz had appeared in a series of quirky roles which didn't rely on her drop-dead-gorgeous good looks. In *The Last Supper*, *She's The One* and *Feeling Minnesota* she was resisting the lure of the easy, romantic roles Hollywood had to offer. Although she succumbed by appearing in Julia Roberts' *My Best Friend's Wedding*, she almost stole the film away from its star name. Her independence of mind made her a good match for Ewan.

Danny Boyle had wanted someone who was 'almost mythically American,' for his leading lady. 'We needed somebody who would respond well to Ewan and his sense of humour.' The team also knew that they needed to have an American star name somewhere in the film if Brad Pitt were not to be playing the lead, being only too aware that Ewan's name alone was not enough to open the film in America.

Diaz was one of five or six candidates for the part, but the first Ewan McGregor knew of her involvement was when he heard she'd won the role. 'I didn't [screen] test with anybody. I didn't know the chemistry would be there between us, but it was, luckily. Because from day one, it was obvious that we were going to have a good time. And I think because we were having such a good time, you can see it on the screen. You can see in our eyes that we're genuinely enjoying each other's company. It heightens all the romance and it heightens all the fun scenes. There were bits that couldn't go in the film because we couldn't stop laughing. She's a really brilliant woman and a lovely lady, Cameron. They say the chemistry between us is very good.'

Perhaps inevitably, speculation turned to how well the pair appeared to be hitting it off in real life. They shared a giant trailer split into two, but were separated only by a wafer-thin wall, which made using the toilet something of a communal experience. Almost as soon as they met, they were thrust together in a series of dance lessons for the fantasy sequences of the film. 'Immediately Ewan and I just hit it off,' Diaz said. 'We went straight to dance rehearsal for four days. So, we got very close, very fast.'

'After Trainspotting, the riskiest thing we could do was an American comedy.'

'It would have been a nightmare if we hadn't,' responded McGregor. 'All that romance stuff was so there, and our eyes were just twinkling away at each other. It would have been impossible to create that with someone you didn't like.' So keen were fans and the press to find out more about Ewan that rumours spread that he was romantically linked with his co-star, despite his marriage and her two-year-old relationship with actor Matt Dillon.

Macdonald wanted to make sure that the cast had the right approach to this film in mind, and as he and Boyle had done on *Trainspotting*, he gave them a handful of films to watch in order to pass on a flavour of the approach to take. Among them was his own grandfather's tale of angelic intervention in human affairs, *A Matter of Life and Death*, and Frank Capra's screwball comedy *It Happened One Night*, with Clark Gable and Claudette Colbert.

All that time spent lying on the floor in front of the television on a Sunday afternoon watching the movie matinees was about to pay off for Ewan. 'I grew up on such films as *It Happened One Night*, which I found particularly valuable because ours shares the road aspect with the guy and girl not remotely knowing each other. And that bang-bang quick-fire dialogue between Clark Gable and Claudette Colbert certainly set the pace. Cameron and I had the same kind of tennis match dialogue to get the rhythm level right.'

'She's a really brilliant woman and a lovely lady,
Cameron. They say the chemistry between us is very
good. All that romance stuff was so there, and our eyes
were just twinkling away at each other.'

Ewan and Cameron Diaz genuinely enjoyed each others company in A Life Less Ordinary.

For Boyle, too, the process of watching these films clarified some of the ideas he was developing: 'A Matter of Life and Death is one of the boldest, most imaginative films I know of. The way it makes the extraordinary and supernatural concrete is something I wanted to achieve in our film. One of the things I learnt from the Capra film – and continued to learn during the editing process – is that in a romantic comedy you can't stray too far from your lead actors, or spend too much time on other strands of the plot. The audience is only really interested in them, and forces you to them when you stray.'

Although not going so far as to compare his leading man to Clark Gable, Boyle did see something of a more contemporary movie star in Ewan's vulnerable, open performance. 'He's got that thing that Tom Hanks has. He's like the guy next door. He's got that ordinariness – that's his nature. He doesn't try to represent himself without spots, and I don't think he's thinking about that. It's instinct. There's something quite naughty about Ewan as well. Very naughty.'

For Ewan, the part of Robert was a great break. It was a chance to be lighter on screen, not as angst-ridden as in Shallow Grave, Trainspotting, The Pillow Book and The Serpent's Kiss. It was a definite change of pace. 'I do tend to be cast as cynical characters,' he admitted ruefully, 'but A Life Less Ordinary is a love story, albeit of an odd sort, and I play a sweet, innocent guy. Everything's going a bit weird for him though, and there's more humour in this than anything I've previously done. Robert and Celine hold up a bank at one point out of some demented innocent madness. Because her father cancels Celine's credit cards, the only solution is to rob a bank. It's that sort of quirkiness we were working with in this light-hearted fantasy.'

As the outsider new to this particular film-making team, Cameron Diaz knew she had some catching up to do, but she was soon a part of the gang. Indeed, occasionally, she and Ewan would be having too good a time, resulting in disruptions to the film's schedule. 'They had to separate us. It was like "You go in that corner and you go in the other corner, you can't play together any more, put down the toys and go to work."'

Pre-production on A Life Less Ordinary had begun about three months before Ewan arrived in Utah. In July 1996, Macdonald, Hodge and Boyle had gathered in Salt Lake City to begin planning their shooting schedule and location scouting. Immediately prior to that, Danny Boyle had been on a coast-to-coast trip across America on his own in a rented car. In an attempt to avoid turning the film into a tourist's view of America, he was keen to familiarise himself with the American heartland. 'John and Andrew are not really into research,' he said of his co-creators. 'I'm obsessed with it, not because I use it a lot but because if you don't use it, you can't throw it away. Prior to that trip I had only been to the East and West coasts, neither of which is really "America".'

On arrival in Salt Lake City, Boyle was reunited with several of the behind-the-scenes team he'd worked with on the previous two films he'd directed, including director of photography Brian Tufano and editor Masahiro Hirakubo. Along with production designer Kave Quinn, he set about compiling a portfolio of visual references he intended to use in preparing the film.

The final weeks of the pre-production were taken up with rehearsals. Here Ewan and Diaz met up with the rest of the film's cast, including Holly Hunter and Delroy Lindo who played the unlikely angels. Macdonald and Boyle had met Hunter at a dinner in Cannes when promoting Trainspotting and had offered her the role. Lindo was much admired by Boyle and seemed ideal casting to contrast with Hunter. Also in the cast were American character actors Dan Hedaya, Stanley Tucci and Maury Chaykin, with British actors Ian McNeice playing a butler and Ian Holm playing Celine's father, the head of the company that Robert works for.

Boyle's rehearsals were less than conventional. Following on from his approach on Shallow Grave, this was more of a getting-to-know-you session than strict line readings and character analysis. Ewan, Diaz and the two angels found themselves packed off to a shooting range in order to learn how to handle and fire the guns that would be central to some of the scenes. Ewan had never fired a gun before – not even on screen – so it was an entirely new experience for him.

In a further attempt to get his leading actors in the right mood for their roles, Boyle took Ewan and Diaz out to a 'red-neck' karaoke bar, similar to the one that would feature in the film. So taken with the atmosphere were they that the two stars took centre stage, performing in front of the bemused customers.

Shooting started on 30 September 1996. A rustic cabin in which Robert and Celine hide out was built in one of the canyons outside the city and rebuilt in the studio for the interior scenes, due to the approaching winter weather – this was especially important as the two leading actors would be nude for some of these scenes. Having such variety of locations on hand and the finance to allow their use was something of a novelty for Boyle. 'It's the first time I've done a great deal of location shooting,' he said. 'In Britain the landscape feels so small and claustrophobic. That's the reason our two previous films were composed almost entirely of interiors.'

Ewan grew to thoroughly dislike the sterile atmosphere of Utah. 'I hated it. Working there was bad enough because you are so high up and all that running around is so hard to do in the very thin air. But the people . . . the Mormons . . . I'd walk to the supermarket with my wife and baby and be stared at because we weren't dressed like them. They looked at me as if I was Satan himself. I have this woolly hat with "Pervert" written on the front and I'd deliberately put it on my daughter's head and walk around just to get a reaction.'

The culture clash with the citizens of Salt Lake City could have been, in itself, a source of great comedy. 'I don't want to offend all of the burghers of Salt Lake City, but it was just a funny place. Quite a conservative area, I think,' Ewan mused, reminded in many ways of the mindset of the older citizens of his home town of Crieff.

He took every opportunity in promotional interviews to knock Utah and Salt Lake City, then suddenly thought twice about what he'd been saying. 'Now I'm worried about being shot by Utah militiamen. Just remember what I told you. If I go there and get shot in the head, just tell them to look for the Utah militia guys.' Although cynical tough guy parts like Alex Law and Mark Renton had put Ewan on the map, within these characters and the others he'd played was a degree of human weakness – whether greed, gullibility or desperation. It was these aspects of his personality that *A Life Less Ordinary* would build upon – he'd be required to do some less than macho things, like burst into an off-the-cuff musical number (shades of *Lipstick on Your Collar)*, wear a less than flattering apron, and cry uncontrollably – as well as dropping his clothes. According to Boyle, Robert was to be a 'quite feminine, emotional part. We tried to undermine a few sexual preconceptions.' Boyle considered Ewan very well suited: 'He's not one of those drop-dead-gorgeous Brad Pitt types, but there's something enormously attractive about him, because he's more human. Most actors want to play macho roles. Ewan loves showing a weakness. Our test audiences show that Americans love a guy who appears to be a loser, even if he isn't really a loser. That's the persona Ewan conveys.'

'I do tend to be cast as cynical characters, but A Life Less Ordinary is a love story, albeit of an odd sort, and I play a sweet, innocent guy.'

Ewan has the ability to turn off and on, avoiding the technique of staying in character through an entire shoot popular with some actors. His American co-stars approached acting rather differently. 'He's quite brilliant,' Ewan said of Delroy Lindo, 'but after every single take, he'll be cursing – Goddamnit – really angry with himself. It's quite funny.' For her part, Cameron Diaz seemed somewhat jealous of Ewan's ability to go in and out of character. 'He makes acting look so easy, he doesn't beat himself up over it.' The shoot wrapped in mid-December, with a reduced unit relocating to Malibu to spend two days shooting at a palatial beach-front house which doubled as Celine's family mansion. After Christmas 1996, post-production was completed back in London.

The risks that *A Life Less Ordinary* took with its form and content – a less than sympathetic leading man, frequent bursts of imaginative whimsy and some decidedly off-beat performances - were exactly the same as those in *Trainspotting*, but they were used by critics as an excuse to lay into the film. Third time out, the unstoppable team of Boyle-Hodge-Macdonald-McGregor had tripped up. *Time* magazine dubbed the film 'reckless, bound to confuse . . . It never leaves well enough, or good enough, alone. It keeps looking – sometimes a little too hard – for ways to transform the ordinary into the discomfiting.' *Entertainment Weekly* went further, calling the film 'so extravagantly misconceived, that it goes off the rails, zooms over the cliff, and crashes into the canyon . . . sometimes, it takes people this talented to misfire this completely.'

With poor reviews, the film gained only a modest audience. An opening weekend in the US in October 1997 of only $2 million led to a final US box office take of $4.2 million to add to the

'What surprises my fans most about me is that
I'm an old married man.'

non-US (including UK) take of $4.7 million. A gross of only $9 million, set against a budget in the region of $12 million made the film a financial failure, even though it had been produced remarkably cheaply. Prime among the film's quirky elements was the animated finale attached. When the finished film underwent a series of test screenings, it was realised that audiences really wanted all the loose ends that had been deliberately left hanging tied up. Boyle believed he had the solution when he suggested an animated sequence to run alongside the film's end credits which would chronicle the further adventures of Robert and Celine.

Boyle commissioned Mike Mort of Passion Pictures to handle this sequence, based on their work on the *Gogs* caveman TV series and their Levi's adverts for British TV. The biggest challenge to Mort and his team of ten animators who worked on the two-minute claymation film for eight weeks was getting the likenesses of the leading actors just right. 'In *Gogs* we never had to worry about realism. The more bizarre our characters looked the better, but for this sequence we needed to continue the action of the movie and characteristics of the movement and design. That was really important if we were to catch the audience's attention.' For many critics and many in the audience, the animated finale would be the highlight of the film.

After pretending to be falling in love with Cameron Diaz during the day, in the evenings Ewan would be back with his wife and daughter. Sometimes Eve and Clara would visit the set, where during breaks from shooting Ewan would spend time entertaining his daughter – and other times she would entertain him. Eve also worked in the art department, and was credited as Art Department Associate on *A Life Less Ordinary*.

He, Eve and Clara had found a house in the hills overlooking Salt Lake City for the duration of shooting. It gave him yet another perspective on Mormon-central. 'It was a weird, yet beautiful place. It has some of the best sky-scapes I've ever seen but the whole town is built in this bowl where you do not have to think about the rest of the world. You are absolutely safe from any normal people. It is built next to this huge, stagnant and stinking lake, which says rather a lot about the people who go to live there. I was pleased to get away from it.'

The consolation was seeing his family every day during shooting. Whether his wife and daughter can come with him has become key to McGregor's decision-making process about which roles to take next. 'I have always made sure they come with me,' he said, realising that his increasingly powerful position in the film industry allowed him now to make this kind of demand of those who sought his services. 'There are too many wrecked marriages in this business for mine to be one, and if anyone doesn't like that, I won't make the film. It's important – I don't want to miss my daughter growing up because of a film. As it is, I'm usually away to work before she's up and back after she's gone to bed. But at least she knows I'm around.'

As a result of spending more time with Eve during the day than with her father, Clara was beginning to speak more French than English – a development which began to worry Ewan. 'She started talking, half in French and half in English. I don't speak French nearly as well as her,' he said, realising that he'd better begin French lessons in order to keep up with his daughter. 'Otherwise, in five years, my daughter will be taking the piss out of me in French and I won't know what she's talking about!'

Utah's strict Mormon drinking laws played havoc with Ewan's hedonistic lifestyle. 'It's pretty common knowledge that I spend half of my free time drinking and the other half dealing with my hangovers,' he said, only half-joking. 'It's not a lifestyle I recommend, but it's mine.' It was to be tough for the actor to keep up his habits in this Mormon stronghold, but he somehow managed it. Determined not to let the local laws interfere with his weekend of relaxation, McGregor managed to live up – or should that be down? – to the stereotype of a Scotsman on a traditional weekend bender. 'They work all week and get pissed on the first day off, then sit at home watching telly all the next day nursing a hangover,' he said of his countrymen. 'One night, I beat director Danny Boyle on the pool table. The next day, he said he couldn't believe it, because I was so drunk I could hardly speak, and yet I was hammering the balls in . . .'

'I'm very, very partial to the margarita, it has to be said,' he cheerfully admitted. 'All my mates drink like bastards. The French drink for pleasure – we just drink.' Ewan was happy to own up to being fascinated by the life and death of actor Richard Burton. He enjoyed hearing stories of how the Welsh actor insisted on shooting no close-ups before 11am, as he'd still be too hungover, or after 2pm, by which time he'd be twelve sheets to the wind again. 'It's very sad,' he said of Burton's fate – and it's this awareness that will probably allow McGregor to avoid a similar downfall. 'No way do I drink like that – I don't drink spirits, necessarily, and I couldn't handle three or four bottles a day. But it fascinates me because it's extreme, and I like extremes.'

Ewan's interest in extremes of behaviour within his own profession have not been reflected in his own attitude to his working life. Coming to fame after working with the low budgets of *Shallow Grave* and *Trainspotting* meant that he wasn't one to demand a bigger trailer, or any of the perks that a star of his stature could easily have in Hollywood. However extraordinary his life was to become, he was resolved to stay as ordinary as possible.

For all their closeness, he and Eve have managed to create for themselves a lifestyle which allows him to pursue his interests, both professionally and personally, while still being part of a stable family unit. 'I like to go out. My wife likes to stay home, but it works out. But she's asleep when I leave to go to the movie set, and I often don't get back till late that night. I think differences work out. Maybe people who are the same shouldn't really live together.'

When he'd finished shooting *A Life Less Ordinary*, Ewan took the opportunity of guest starring in one of his favourite TV shows, making the most of his contacts in America. *E.R.* - which stands for Emergency Room, the casualty department in an American hospital – had been created by writer and film-maker Michael Crichton for Steven Spielberg's Amblin company and had debuted on NBC in 1995 to instant acclaim and ratings-topping success. *E.R.* had made a star of George Clooney, who later switched to the movies playing the third Batman in the dire *Batman and Robin*. *E.R.* was known for featuring interesting actors in guest-starring roles.

For McGregor there was only one reason for doing the show: 'Because I love *E.R.* – I just love it. I wanted to see myself amongst those people I know so well from television, and it was great fun,' he admitted. Through his agent he made his interest in appearing on the show clear to the producers, who were only too glad to snap him up and draft an episode around him. His episode, 'The Long Way Around', directed by Christopher Chulack, was recorded in Chicago in January 1997.

Ewan played Duncan, a young Scot staying with his American cousin. The pair set out to hold up a convenience store and one of the *E.R.* nurses, Carol Hathaway (Julianna Margulies) gets caught up in the mayhem that ensues. As Hathaway and Duncan bond, the course is set for tragedy as Duncan attempts to escape from the police. It's a claustrophobic piece with most of the action taking place within the confines of the convenience store and Hathaway being the sole *E.R.* character featured at any length. Where most *E.R.* episodes are ensemble, soap opera-like pieces, 'The Long Way Around' was a much more theatrical endeavour, concentrating on character. It turned out to be a great showcase for Ewan and a clever way of advertising the forthcoming release of *A Life Less Ordinary* to prime-time TV viewers across America.

'He's not one of those drop-dead gorgeous Brad Pitt types, but there's something enormously attractive about him, because he's more human.' Danny Boyle on Ewan.

The episode climaxes with Duncan being brought into the *E.R.* by Nurse Hathaway, mortally wounded. He dies on the table as the *E.R.* staff rally round to save him. Although he didn't work with many of the cast other than Julianna Margulies for long, as a fan of the show Ewan was keen to meet and chat with George Clooney and Anthony Edwards. He was disappointed to discover that Clooney's unique eyes-down acting style stemmed from the fact that he was looking down to read his lines written out on bed sheets and in other concealed places.

It wasn't the first time Ewan had managed to meet his idols. Prime among the celebrities he was happy to hang out with were Deborah Harry, late of Blondie, and the Gallagher brothers from Oasis, McGregor's favourite band. 'I've met them both now, Liam and Noel, they were so sweet you wouldn't believe it. And me and Ewen Bremner [co-star of *Trainspotting*] got to introduce them at the MTV Awards. We weren't there at all, really, we did it from MTV Camden. That's probably top secret.' Knowing that people he was a fan of were as ordinary as he was helped him come to terms with his own fame. But he remained less than comfortable with the three-ring circus that had grown up around him. 'I have moments when I'm anxious and I'm trying to figure what I'm anxious about.'

However, there was more to come, though not without a domestic crisis first.

CHAPTER 8

THE GOLDEN YEARS

WRAPPING HIS AMERICAN ADVENTURES EARLY IN 1997, Ewan realised he'd been working non-stop for over two years. While he had admitted to being driven, this was a ridiculous pace of work for a recently married man with a young daughter.

He made up his mind upon returning to London that he'd take the first quarter of 1997 off work altogether and spend time with his family. It was intended to be a quiet, non-dramatic time at home, but Ewan had no sooner got home than a serious illness struck Clara and all thought of relaxation was lost.

For his role on *E.R.* Ewan had broken his rule of always having his family on location with him. Eve and Clara had remained in London while he'd recorded his guest appearance on the medical soap opera. He'd got back to London to find Clara in hospital, suffering from meningitis. The illness, which affects the brain, is potentially fatal in young children.

'I've always had a desperate desire to be a rock star.'

Eve had become worried by her daughter's condition – Clara's temperature was rising and she was listless and unresponsive. Faced with a decision, Eve decided to take Clara into Chelsea and Westminster hospital. 'She did brilliantly,' said Ewan of his wife's quick thinking. 'If it had been 24 hours later, it would have been too late.'

Ewan flew back from the United States as soon as he heard Clara was ill. 'My daughter almost died and I wasn't there to help,' he said, expressing the deep guilt he felt at being away from home at such a crucial time. 'By the time I got there all I saw was little grey baby with tubes up her nose, wired to a heart machine.'

Clara was hospitalised for weeks and there was little Ewan or Eve could do but sit by her bedside and wait. It was a gruelling time for the couple, made worse by press intrusions. Spending a day at home, Ewan was doorstepped by a journalist from the *News of the World*, desperate for a comment from the star on his daughter's chance of surviving the deadly disease.

'He said: "I want to ask you about Clara" and I just took his fucking head off,' recalled the actor. This was a defining moment in Ewan's relations with the British press. From the beginning of his career he had enjoyed giving interviews, liking nothing more than to talk about himself, his hangovers and, more recently, his wife and child. What he didn't like was when the press came after him uninvited, looking for some kind of non-existent scandal. It was that kind of reporting that had led to speculation about his relationship with Cameron Diaz during the shooting of *A Life Less Ordinary*.

Now he was being doorstepped as his daughter's life hung in the balance. Refusing to comment, he angrily slammed the door in the reporter's face. From then on Ewan would be less than co-operative with the British tabloid press when it came to interviews, having come to the conclusion that it would be impossible to keep them away from his private life.

Clara recovered quickly, but her illness and the fear her parents had felt put Ewan's globe-trotting movie star lifestyle into perspective. 'It was the scariest, but also the happiest thing that ever happened to me, because she came through it.'

The incident with Clara also put some strain on the relationship between Ewan and Eve – it was the first crisis they had faced. 'Eve dealt with it in her own way and so did I, which was a mistake,' he admitted, over a year after the event. 'We should have done it together. You can't just breeze through those kind of events – there are a lot of feelings that have to be dealt with and thrashed out afterwards. We have had a lot of talking to do over this last summer.'

He was convinced that when his daughter had fallen ill while he was shooting *E.R.*, she'd reacted badly to the fact that 'Daddy' wasn't there. 'Afterwards she was a wee bit weird with me,' he confided. 'On reflection I would rather not have gone [to do *E.R.*].'

Ewan's resolution to put family before work was welcomed by Eve. The couple felt they could each continue to develop their careers at a more relaxed pace while both taking responsibility for Clara's welfare. Eve had kept up her own professional commitments, and soon after Clara's illness she spent some time away on business, leaving Ewan to spend time with his daughter on a family trip to see her grandparents in Crieff. It was an important time for him – he felt he was making things up with his daughter after being absent when she became ill.

It was this nurturing, almost feminine side of the laddish film star that had appeared in both *A Life Less Ordinary* and *E.R.* 'Men now are supposed to be soft and cry, yet still be tough. So, basically we just flummox about, being beaten by women all over the place. The Scots are quite an emotional race; my mother will cry at the drop of a hat, usually with joy though. I cry easily, too, and so does my dad, but in America men appear to feel the need to be more macho. That's partly why British actors seem more interesting to them.'

His next film role was certainly to remove any macho image that he might have.

By March 1997 Ewan was ready to go back to work. His return to film-making was in Todd Haynes's *Velvet Goldmine*, a colourful celebration of the British 'glam rock' era of the early seventies, a musical-lifestyle-fashion movement driven by such stars as David Bowie, Bryan Ferry and Marc Bolan. Sexual ambiguity and playing with notions of identity and look were as central to glam rock as the music, and performers like Bowie would adopt and discard identities rapidly.

Haynes had been keen on the subject since the late eighties and had been commissioned to write a script in 1994 by UK producers Zenith. 'The early seventies was just an extraordinary time, and it seemed such an overlooked period,' said Haynes. 'I'm very interested in topics for my films that call notions of identity into question.'

Haynes's long-time producer Christine Vachon agreed that the glam rock era was about more than just the music. 'What was so interesting about that brief time,' she said, 'is that not only was it OK to experiment with gender, you had to in order to be musically successful. When you see some old *Top of the Pops* shows from that time, even bands like the Rolling Stones, who weren't associated with glam rock, wore lipstick and feather boas. The whole movement was fascinating. In the end it went as far as it could. It was almost too dangerous.'

Haynes had courted controversy with his film debut in 1987, a 43-minute short video entitled *Superstar: The Karen Carpenter Story* which told of the singer's life, battle with anorexia and death with the use of Barbie doll figures filmed against cardboard cut out sets. Karen's brother Richard Carpenter and A&M Records succeeded in getting distribution of the film halted, although bootleg copies have circulated widely.

Haynes followed that with *Poison*, a feature-length trilogy of stories about sexual obsession and crime, inspired by the works of Jean Genet. As it was partly funded with $25,000 of public money from the National Endowment for the Arts, the controversy this time surrounded whether such material should receive any public subsidy at all. A screening of the film at the 1991 Sundance Film Festival was greeted with outrage and walkouts, although the worst that could be said about *Poison* is that it is rather boring.

Haynes finally fulfilled his promise in 1995 with *Safe*, an eco-fable starring the excellent Julianne Moore as a well-off San Fernando housewife who suffers from a mysterious series of allergies, perhaps reflecting a reaction against life in the twentieth century. Although baffled by the film, many critics placed it on their Top Ten lists for the year.

Haynes has said that much of his work has indirectly been about the scourge of AIDS, and although there's no direct reference, the era of glam rock is seen in *Velvet Goldmine* as a time of freedom and experiment before the disease brought it all to an end. 'There was something about the time that opened up, then closed back down again quickly in terms of cultural groups,' Haynes claimed. 'In the early seventies, there were black and white communities interested in each other, in things we all shared. By the eighties, it was a conservative climate of fearfulness, which emphasised our differences.'

Haynes wasn't setting out in *Velvet Goldmine* to make a documentary but a fictional celebration of an era he looked back to with a certain degree of longing. 'It takes to heart the spirit of glam rock, which is not about telling the truth, but dressing it up. I wanted the film to have a fictional freedom about it – I didn't want it to be locked into the weight of what really happened. It's not a naturalistic experience, and it shouldn't be – it's glam rock.'

Modelled on *Citizen Kane*, the narrative of *Velvet Goldmine* (which was produced by Michael Stipe of REM) begins in the conservative, bleak and bland eighties with Arthur Stuart (Christian Bale, *Empire of the Sun*), a British journalist working on a New York newspaper, setting out to uncover the true story of Brian Slade (Jonathan Rhys-Meyers), a flamboyant, charismatic, Bowie-like seventies rock star who has faked his own assassination because he is unable to escape from his created persona.

In tried and tested rock biopic rise-and-fall fashion, Arthur tracks down Mandy (Toni Collette, who starred with Ewan in *Emma*), Slade's wife. In flashbacks she reveals Slade's true story, including his infatuation with American singer Curt Wild (played by Ewan). 'I was reading Oscar Wilde and reading about glam rock at the same time,' Haynes noted of some of his influences. The film's title, which comes from an obscure David Bowie out-take from 1971, had to convey something of the nature of the subject. 'I loved the name,' he said of the Bowie track. 'It's tactile and colourful and evocative, and it has the mysteriousness and seductiveness I want the film to have.'

'I cry easily, and so does my dad, but in America men appear to feel the need to be more macho. That's partly why British actors seem more interesting to them.'

Ewan was aware of Haynes's previous work and knew that his playing with his gender on screen would be in safe and competent hands. 'I loved *Safe*,' he said. 'I thought it was an amazing movie. This one was an amazing piece of writing.'

Being asked to take one of the prime roles in *Velvet Goldmine* would be the fulfilment of another of Ewan's childhood dreams. 'I play an American rock'n'roll star who comes to work in England and meets a sticky end. I wear lots of long bleached blond wigs, leather trousers and hipster flares. I'm quite grungy. It's the other actors who look high camp. My character isn't based on anyone in particular, but I did watch Iggy Pop videos to get his incredible moves down.'

Ever since his school days as the drummer in the short-lived Scarlet Pride Ewan had dreamed of rock'n'roll stardom. Now, he could strut his stuff as a rock'n'roll legend, albeit a fictional one from a time of which he was blissfully ignorant. 'I always had a desperate desire to be a rock star and, I thought, if I played one I'd get over it, but it seems to have had the reverse affect.'

Haynes agreed that Ewan's desire actually to be a real-life rock star comes across in his performance. 'Ewan was wonderful. I think it fulfilled a lot of the age-old desire to be a rock star that most of us have, but would be unable to execute with such power. He also sang live, did unbelievably strenuous, outrageous performances and gave 100 per cent consistently in every take, while allowing the performance to feel raw and spontaneous.'

Ewan had to throw himself about on stage, in a small studio twenty miles outside of London. Todd said, "There's a field, an open-air concert, and it's full of hippies." I come on doing all this stuff and they boo me and tell me to get off. And he said just moon at them at the end of "TV Eye".

'But I remember this thing where Iggy just undid his pants, stood with his hand down the front of his trousers for ages, just staring them out. And started jiggling about, and his pants started to move down slowly . . . So I did this and started to pull my willy about and told them to fuck off. It came out of nowhere and there was a dead silence after he said "Cut!" But I had to do it again and again all night long from all different angles, so they must have liked it.'

'It's great to be there at 4am in front of 400 extras getting paid well for doing something that would normally end you up in prison.'

One particularly memorable sequence is a 'falling-in-love' montage between Wild and Slade, acted out to Lou Reed's 'Satellite of Love'. Part of it involves them cavorting on a recreation of a fairground rocket ride constructed in the studio. Ewan also worked very hard on a concert sequence recorded at the London music venue Brixton Academy, finally making his dreams of performing in front of a screaming audience come true.

'I play an American rock 'n' roll star who comes . . .

Ewan fulfilling his rock 'n' roll stardom dreams in Velvet Goldmine, *and far right with co-star Jonathan Rhys-Myers.*

. . . to work in England and meets a sticky end.'

Although Ewan had been dogged by speculation about affairs with co-stars, he'd never been thought of as potentially in-the-closet, unlike some other young stars whose sexuality has been much speculated about. Despite Ewan's willingness to disrobe on screen and play bisexual characters like Jerome in *The Pillow Book*, his own sexuality was firmly on record. It was with this background that he felt secure in tackling the sex scenes required by *Velvet Goldmine*.

'I have gay love scenes with Christian Bale, and there's a funny story about that,' he said, recalling a flashback sequence when the American pop star meets the teenaged Arthur Stuart at a concert. 'I come offstage and he's in the wings there, and I take him up onto this rooftop and we have sex. It's this rooftop in King's Cross, and Christian and I are both straight guys, trying not to make too big a deal about this. And we were actually giving it full legs, which was brilliant. But it was going on for a very long time, I thought, with nobody yelling, "Cut!" Like, "God, I'd never be going on this long with a girl . . ."'

'But I kept going, kept going, kept going, and by this time we're going so quick there was hair flying round and moaning sounds. And people on the street are going, "What the fuck's going on there?" Finally, I said, "Well, I'm gonna look," because Christian couldn't figure it out either. And I looked on the rooftop and people were picking up the tracks, and cables and wires. They just never said, "Cut." They hadn't bothered to stop us. Bastards.'

The finished film is a kaleidoscope of colours, music and images, strung together in a very loose investigative narrative. At two hours and five minutes, it outstays its welcome, but it proves an effective recreation of a gaudy era, albeit through the eyes of a film-maker who didn't experience any of it first hand. Packed with glittering musical numbers, and especially brought to life whenever top-billed McGregor is on screen, *Velvet Goldmine* was as over-the-top and inconsequential as glam rock itself.

Its premiere was at Cannes in the summer of 1998, where it was awarded a Special Jury Prize for Artistic Contribution. *Variety* called the film 'constantly imaginative, stylistically lively, but dramatically inert'. However, Ewan escaped the criticisms of the reviewer, Todd McCarthy, who noticed Slade's 'career-altering encounter with the outlandish American singer Curt Wild (Ewan McGregor), whose audacious act (including rude posturing, full frontal nudity and diving through flames into the audience) makes Slade realise he's seen the future. McGregor's ejaculatory performance in this number is amazing, fully convincing as the Iggy Pop-like maniac he's supposed to be.'

Ewan made a public appearance to support the film for its opening gala screening at the Edinburgh International Film Festival on Sunday 16 August 1998 at the city's Odeon cinema, just after doing duty as the chieftain at Crieff Highland Games. Jonathan Rhys Meyers was also supposed to attend, but due to an airline foul-up he missed the event. *Velvet Goldmine* went on to a wider release in the UK and US later in the autumn of 1998.

Just prior to the film's official release, it was suggested that Ewan's rock'n'roll dreams might come true away from the movie screen. It appeared that some record label executives had been so impressed by his vocal duties on *Velvet Goldmine* that they thought he might like to record an album to tie in with the film. This was déjà vu for Ewan, bringing to mind *Lipstick on Your Collar*. Although he did re-record the vocals on three numbers for a soundtrack album, as a fan of Oasis Ewan felt it wasn't wise to launch a pop career with an album of glam rock covers.

Velvet Goldmine's costumer Sandy Powell, responsible for the now-antique costumes featured in the movie, was convinced that a glam rock revival was just around the corner, even though the clothes had been hard to find. 'All the sequinned stuff and satin have disintegrated and worn away, but the horrible frumpy polyester and the synthetics have survived!'

For his part, Ewan McGregor was not impressed by the thought of a glam rock revival. 'I hope not,' he cringed, 'because it's really annoying music. But fashion-wise, you drive through Camden [in north London] and there are people there wearing more outrageously seventies clothes than we wear in this film. It's a huge statement to make, but I'm not into all that. We definitely shouldn't go back to wearing flowery shirts and flares – they look ridiculous. It seems a bit sad to me.'

The early part of 1997 had again been a busy one. Just before beginning work on *Velvet Goldmine*, Ewan had made a return trip to his old school, Morrison's Academy in Crieff, where he'd been invited to speak to the pupils and lead a drama class. It was an invitation he couldn't resist.

He turned up at the school for assembly first thing in the morning, where he gingerly joined in with the hymn-singing before being introduced by Rector Gareth Edwards. A press conference followed, at which Ewan answered a handful of questions and posed with some of the school's current pupils for photos.

Then it was down to business – an interview in the sixth form common room for the school yearbook conducted by a handful of giggling teenagers. Following his Q&A, McGregor gave a lecture to the pupils of the fifth and sixth years about his work in the film industry and how his career had developed. He also told pupils he was keen to work with Billy Connolly and Sean Connery. That afternoon he conducted a drama workshop with pupils who were preparing for a production of *Tom Sawyer*.

It was an interesting day for Ewan, to return so soon, in such a different capacity, after having left the school under an academic cloud. It was an even more amazing day for the pupils, many of whom were fans. One, writing in the school magazine, noted that Ewan was 'the idol of thousands, yet he remains a genuine charmer'.

His charm was more widely recognised during the same period, as he scooped a series of coveted awards in a very short period of time. In February 1997 he was recognised as the Best Film Actor by the Variety Club Showbusiness Awards and was voted Scotland's Film Personality of the Year in the same week by readers of the *Daily Record*, winning out over the inevitable Sean Connery, Oscar-winner Peter Capaldi and TV star Robbie Coltrane.

Then in March he shared the Best Actor Award from the London Critics' Circle with Sir Ian McKellan, and was declared Best Actor in the *Empire* magazine awards (for the third consecutive year). In total, *Trainspotting* walked off with four *Empire* Awards, including Best Film, Best Director and Best British Newcomer for Ewen Bremner.

By December of 1997 his string of awards would be complete when the Scottish BAFTAs awarded *Trainspotting* the Best Film accolade and saw Ewan crowned as Best Actor. It had been a heady time for Ewan as the critical recognition of his work in *Trainspotting* filtered through into the various 'year's best' awards.

Following his visit to Morrison's Academy, a previous and little seen TV appearance popped up on Sky, Britain's satellite TV service. 'The Cold War' was an episode of the *Tales from the Crypt* horror anthology series produced by Home Box Office. Shot in London in 1995, 'The Cold War' starred Ewan alongside Jane Horrocks (who was later to feature with him in the British film *Little Voice*). He played an American zombie in London who, with his girlfriend (Horrocks), goes around robbing stores, while complaining about England. The slight drama concludes when the zombies meet up with and battle a vampire who has taken a shine to Horrocks.

Screened simply because of Ewan's rising fame rather than because it was a good episode, 'The Cold War' was a rent-paying job Ewan had tackled around the same time as he'd made *Kavanagh QC* for ITV. He had also done a walk-on part at about the same time in *Karaoke*, one of the pair of posthumously-produced dramas written by Dennis Potter. 'I did it because Dennis gave me my first break,' Ewan said of his brief return to television.

A year after his return visit in February 1997, Ewan and Morrison's Academy were back in the news again – in a slightly less flattering capacity. In February 1998, the school launched an appeal to raise £1 million to refurbish and upgrade the buildings that Ewan's great-great-grandfather James had helped construct in 1860.

Some of the pupils, who'd been impressed with Ewan's visit the previous year, decided to write to the star in the hope that he could help, either through a personal donation or by making an appearance at a fund-raising event. However, the pressure of his film-making schedule prevented him from getting involved, although this was reported – by the tabloid press that he was growing to despise – as simple minded meanness on his part.

Rector Gareth Edwards was happy to set the record straight, although he was disappointed that 'old boy' McGregor couldn't help out with the fund-raising. 'Ewan has been good to the school in the past,' he said, 'and we are all proud of him. He gave us a day out of his schedule at a very busy time for him last year to come and talk to the pupils. The school's profile has already been raised because of the connection with him.'

Edwards also had something to add to the many profiles that were appearing in newspapers which exaggerated Ewan's childhood exploits, turning him into some sort of punk rebel tearaway who'd terrorised Crieff. 'He is often portrayed as somewhat of a rebel,' said Edwards, 'but he was not by any means a rebel at school. He was a very good pupil.'

It was to be as a 'good pupil' with a difference that he next appeared on screen.

'I wear lots of long bleached blonde wigs, leather trousers and hipster flares . . .

As a result of his role in Velvet Goldmine *Ewan was offered but turned down the opportunity to record a glam rock album.*

. . . I'm quite grungy . . . I watched Iggy Pop videos to get his incredible moves down.'

CHAPTER 9

USE THE FORCE

D URING MOST OF THE SHOOTING OF *VELVET GOLDMINE*, Ewan McGregor was working under the burden of a secret he could reveal to no-one. He had heard, in 1997, that he was set to follow his uncle, Denis Lawson, into space and become part of a twenty-year-old science fiction legend. The phone call had come through from his agent Lindy King (who had gone with her client to a new agency, Peter, Frasers and Dunlop), during the first day of shooting in March 1997. He was naturally delighted to hear he'd been cast in the role of Obi Wan Kenobi in the *Star Wars* prequel trilogy, but he was put under oath not to let anyone else in on the secret until the official announcement, due two months later. 'I told my wife,' he admitted during the Scottish People's Film Festival in early 1998. 'And I told my parents, that was it. I didn't tell anyone else for a long while. When I first got the *Star Wars* prequel, I did honestly think "Maybe this is not the right thing for me to do." Then I went through a stage where I couldn't even think about it. I was kind of in *Star Wars* denial.'

During that first day of shooting on *Velvet Goldmine*, Ewan couldn't stop smiling. All day people working on the film kept asking him if he was all right and there was nothing he could say to explain the cheesy grin he was sporting. Perhaps, people thought, he was just enjoying the flamboyant clothes he was getting to wear in his over-the-top role?

'It was quite a day, knowing that I'd got it and couldn't tell anyone. It was hard,' he said. He'd been in the running for the role for a while, and his name had been repeatedly connected with a new series of *Star Wars* films long before their existence was even officially confirmed. 'I met the casting director about a year before I got the role. We had a meeting, then about a year later – almost to the day – I went back and met her again. Then I met George Lucas [director of the new film and the original 1977 *Star Wars*] and Rick McCallum [producer of the new films]. Then I screen tested with Liam Neeson. Then I got offered the job.'

'I think of Star Wars movies as being rather unique. I don't see them just as studio blockbusters.'

Isobel Thomas worked as a personal assistant to George Lucas during his time at Leavesden, where the new film would shoot, and she recalled Ewan's top secret screen test: 'He's great, totally unaffected by success. He was nervous when he came for the screen test, which certainly helped me be more relaxed with him.'

Ewan's co-star in the film was to be Liam Neeson, best-known for his role as Oskar Schindler in Steven Spielberg's *Schindler's List*, but he had previously featured in such dramatic films as *Michael Collins*, *Rob Roy*, *The Big Man* and *The Mission*. He'd been cast in the first *Star Wars* prequel as a wise Jedi knight who would be responsible for training the young Obi Wan Kenobi in the ways of the Force, in much the same way as Luke Skywalker had been taught by the elderly Kenobi in *Star Wars*.

For Ewan, stepping into the legendary *Star Wars* universe was to be an amazing experience. 'A man from props came up and took me into the room. There were 60 guys standing about and he came out, dead secretive, with this big wooden box with two padlocks on, and the secrecy was incredible. He unlocked it, asked me if I was ready, and inlaid in black felt there were these nine or ten light sabre handles. And I just about really *shat* myself. And I took out these precious things and chose my handle and realised how much these things were ingrown in the psyche. I grew up on them. "Dad, I've broken me light sabre again!"'

The *Star Wars* movies had begun as the dream of teenager George Lucas in the late fifties. Born in Modesto, California in 1944, Lucas had grown up like many other kids of the period. His

father, George Snr, ran a stationery store, where Lucas would help out. However, his mother, Dorothy, was often ill and under the care of his two sisters.

Fanatically interested in cars, he first got one of his own – 'a very small Fiat' – at the age of sixteen. This interest would be behind his Oscar-winning nostalgic movie *American Graffiti*. But his obsession with cars and speed nearly led to a fatal road accident, just days before he was due to graduate from high school. On Tuesday 12 June 1962 he was racing his prized Fiat along a quiet rural road through the walnut groves at the back of his home. The area was a notorious blackspot with a history of fatalities, but that knowledge didn't stop him from speeding.

The car collided with a Chevrolet Impala, driven by another local teenager, which hit his Fiat from the side. Lucas's car was sent crashing into the trees, flipping over before coming to rest. The seat belt in the car snapped and Lucas was thrown through a hole in the car's roof, while the vehicle ended up wrapped around a tree.

He had escaped the crash with his life, but the injuries he sustained included crushed lungs, which led to a period of four months' recovery. The time he was confined to bed gave him a new perspective on the life he'd very nearly lost that June evening. It also gave him plenty of time to pursue some of his other passions – comic books like *Batman* and *Superman* and watching science fiction serials from the thirties on television, including his favourite, *Flash Gordon Conquers the Universe*. Pondering why he'd survived the crash, Lucas began to lay the foundations for the mythology which would underlie the blockbusting *Star Wars* movie trilogy.

After two years at college, Lucas moved to Los Angeles and studied film-making at the University of Southern California. He made a series of prize-winning shorts, among them one called *THX* which he later expanded as his debut film, the crisp science fiction thriller *THX 1138*, which starred Robert Duvall. Although strikingly original and visually experimental, Lucas's 1971 feature film debut didn't set the world of Hollywood alight.

That honour was reserved for his second movie, the warmly nostalgic *American Graffiti* (1973). Set among a group of fifties teenagers, the film brought to life Lucas's own youth in Modesto, featuring cars, racing, girls and music. It featured a series of actors who would go on to make a splash in later movies, including Harrison Ford, Ron Howard and Richard Dreyfuss (who played the Lucas figure in the drama). It was an idealised account, of course, but the film made a huge impact. Nearly broke when he started filming, after *American Graffiti* came out in August 1973 Lucas was not only a millionaire (the film netted him $4 million after taxes) but also a celebrity. He was only 28.

'When I first got the Star Wars prequel, I did honestly think "Maybe this is not the right thing for me to do." Then I went through a stage where I couldn't even think about it. I was kind of in Star Wars denial.'

Even before the success of *American Graffiti*, George Lucas had confided in a few friends – among them *Godfather* director Francis Ford Coppola – his desire to make a new version of *Flash Gordon*, the series of exciting space adventures he'd loved so much in childhood. The ideas had been developing in his mind since his teenage car crash. His movie would be *Flash Gordon* crossed with a Japanese samurai epic (he loved Japanese cinema and at one stage even contemplated making his space movie with an all-Japanese cast) with a hefty dose of the swashbuckling adventure of Errol Flynn movies and pirate films like *Captain Blood*. The only problem now was writing a script.

Lucas had so many ideas, concepts and characters for the film, which in 1974 he was calling *The Star Wars*, that he ended up splitting his movie into three, thereby creating an epic trilogy. Pre-production of the first began in 1975 on what was to be a $3.5 million movie. However, Lucas was faced with creating a universe from scratch. It was all right to pretend Tunisia was the alien planet of Tatooine, but how on earth was the director going to create the spectacular space battles which he envisaged as being like the fast-moving Spitfire dog fights from Battle of Britain movies?

The answer was to be Industrial Light and Magic (ILM), a new special effects operation which Lucas himself created and recruited for. Comprising a host of wayward talents, ILM would go on to change the face of movie making and special effects. In the mid-seventies, though, they were desperately trying to realise Lucas's vision of *Star Wars*, for which the budget steadily climbed to $7 million, then $9.5 million and finally $12.5 million when production finally wrapped. The experience proved to be a defining one for the film-maker – it both created his future meal ticket, but also put him off ever directing a movie again, such had been the strain on his personal health, mental well-being and his marriage.

Star Wars quickly became a phenomenon after its release in May 1977, even though the studio, 20th Century Fox, didn't know what they had, thinking it was a B-movie whose production had got out of control. When making the production deal with Fox, Lucas had shrewdly hung onto the rights to the characters, any sequels and all merchandising rights. Fox weren't too bothered, thinking the film would disappear without a trace. The movie had only really been promoted to science fiction fans through conventions and fan newsletters, so everyone was stunned at the queues which formed at cinemas as word-of-mouth spread about just what a blast this movie was.

The film introduced the world to Luke Skywalker, Darth Vader and the bickering androids C3PO and R2-D2. It served as a launch pad for the career of Harrison Ford, and also provided a nice little pension for character actor Alec Guinness who, in an echo of Lucas's own negotiating style, had won himself two percentage points of the film's gross income rather than a one-off fee to play the venerable Jedi Knight, Obi Wan Kenobi. Guiness made millions from the film.

In time, *Star Wars'* two sequels appeared – *The Empire Strikes Back*, a darker fable of revenge from 1980 which revealed something of the trilogy's familial relationships, and, in 1983, *Return of the Jedi*, a much lighter romp which brought a form of redemption for the series' main villain, Darth Vader. And that was that, apart from a huge merchandising empire. There were to be no more *Star Wars* movies, despite early talk from Lucas that as *Star Wars* was billed as Episode Four there would be another two trilogies, one from before the three movies already made and one after, featuring the original cast as older versions of the characters.

However, the fans clung to the dream of seeing the rest of the epic and, as the twentieth anniversary of the original film approached in 1997, rumour was rife that Lucas was about to begin work on one of the outstanding trilogies. In the intervening years he may not have directed another film but he had created a film-making empire like no other, built largely around ILM. Moreover, as well as concentrating on developing new film-making technologies, he had produced a variety of movies – among them the Steven Spielberg's *Raiders of the Lost Ark* and its sequels, fantasy adventures *Labyrinth* and *Howard the Duck*, and dramas like Coppola's *Tucker: The Man and his Dream*. But Lucas would not embark on a new series of *Star Wars* films until he had the technology to tell the rest of his epic story in a truly awe-inspiring cinematic fashion.

Lucas knew he wouldn't have a new film ready for the anniversary, so both as a 'thank you' to the fans of the first three movies and as a test of some of the technology he'd been developing, he released the *Star Wars Trilogy Special Editions* in 1997, restoring the prints and adding new digital-computer generated characters and effects. As these revamped versions of the originals were unspooling at cinemas around the world, he was looking for a star for his new *Star Wars*.

In 1977 Ewan McGregor was six years old. He'd been blown away by *Star Wars*, almost as much by the fact that his Uncle Denis was flying an X-Wing as by the stirring story and stunning special effects. Although he didn't have many of them, Ewan would spend hours over the next few years playing with his little *Star Wars* action figures. Twenty years later, standing on the set of the first episode of a new *Star Wars* trilogy in the heart of the Leavesden countryside, he reflected that he was going to become one of those action figures.

Although he was on record for his vehement dislike of blockbuster American movies like *Independence Day* – and they don't come much bigger than the *Star Wars* franchise – Ewan was happy to make an exception. 'A film like *Independence Day*', he reiterated his disdain, 'that's what I hate – those are the people who don't deserve to be making movies. *Star Wars* is a completely different ballgame. Those movies stand on their own, they're unique. They're legends, they're kind of modern fables – they were for me as a kid. They're not studio product, they're Lucas's pictures – he does them on his own and then sells them to Fox or whatever. They don't go through a committee of eighteen screenwriters – he writes them. And they don't get screen-tested.'

Late in 1996 the *Star Wars* circus had arrived in Britain. Lucas had made the original three films at EMI Elstree Studios, but for the first of the new trilogy he chose Leavesden, a former Rolls-Royce car factory which had been converted into a modern high-tech studio complex for the James Bond movie *GoldenEye*. With over half a million square feet of studio space and a backlot of 100 acres it was the ideal base.

Lucas would shoot again in Tunisia, as much of his new *Star Wars: The Phantom Menace* (as Lucasfilm officially dubbed the movie in autumn 1998) would take place on the planet Tatooine, and in Italy at Caserta Royal Palace, as well as at Leavesden. All of the film-making technology that Lucas had developed over the past twenty years would be brought to bear on this new production, which was to feature everything from computer-generated characters to digitally-created sets, vehicles, weapons and landscapes.

Lucas hired producer Rick McCallum to co-ordinate the new film. McCallum had worked extensively on *The Young Indiana Jones Chronicles* television series, where Lucas had tried out many of his new computer graphics techniques, and had been responsible for bringing the revamped *Star Wars Trilogy Special Editions* to the big screen.

Despite the lasting impact of *Star Wars*, Lucas was nervous about returning to the series – both personally as director, but also in terms of whether the audience would be as interested in the new movies as they were in the originals. 'The big chance I'm taking is that I'm working on something that I started twenty years ago and whether it will fit into the modern world marketing-wise, I'm not sure,' he confessed. 'The first one is very much like *Star Wars*, it's kind of upbeat and fun. The first one always gets to introduce the characters and doesn't have all that much else to do, so it's easy. Second one, things start to go wrong and get complicated, and the third one is the dark one – it'll probably fit really well with the 21st century.'

Set 40 years before *Star Wars*, the new trilogy of movies picks up on the activities of younger versions of some of the characters audiences already know. Child actor Jake Lloyd won the role of Anakin Skywalker, the youngster who is fated to grow up and become the villainous Darth Vader. Also featured are Ian McDiarmid as Senator Palpatine, who later becomes the Galactic Emperor (the part he played in *Return of the Jedi*), and well-known actors Liam Neeson and Samuel L. Jackson as a pair of Jedi Knights.

The new $80 million addition to the *Star Wars* universe opens with a powerful army launching a bid to conquer the Old Republic, with the planet of Tatooine being one of the first to fall. Following the murder of his mother and sister, Anakin Skywalker (Lloyd) is recruited by the planet's conquerors, until he is rescued by trainee Jedi Knight Obi Wan Kenobi (Ewan) and his guru (Neeson). Together the trio battle to save the Old Republic and the film climaxes with an epic conflict on a planet mainly composed of water.

Ewan was aware of the problems of following someone as well-known as and as distinctive as Alec Guinness. 'It was really exciting to be able to play someone who's legendary,' said McGregor. 'I had to play Alec Guinness's character as a young man, so I mainly worked on his voice. I was trying to take his voice, which is very, very distinct and put it into a young person's body, which is quite weird. I don't know if it worked or not, because the voice doesn't age very much. There's not that great difference in the sound of your voice when you're in your thirties or in your fifties. I'm using a voice that I recognise as an old man's voice and I don't know if that's going to work out.'

During production George Lucas made plain his reasons for selecting Ewan as the hero. 'He's the perfect young Harrison Ford,' the director claimed, revealing that Ewan would be at the centre of much of the action, 'but he's also the perfect young Alec Guinness. He's extremely relaxed and very strong – all the things that Alec Guinness is.'

One of the first visitors to the set at Leavesden when filming began in June 1997 was Denis Lawson. He'd been invited to lunch by Ewan, and when he met George Lucas again for the first time since *Return of the Jedi* in 1983 he claimed that Lucas was still wearing the same checked shirt.

It was coming across the sight of the droid R2-D2 in a props room at Leavesden that really brought home to Ewan what was happening. 'When I first met R2-D2 I almost went down on the ground. I walked into the props room and there were about fifty prop-makers and I was just going "Aahhhh". They all knew how I felt.' But when he returned home that night and told Eve

'I thought a film about traders must be very dull, but infact it's an incredible story and not the kind of part I've played before, so it's good.'

Ewan (Nick Leeson) and Anna Friel (Lisa Leeson) in Rogue Trader.

that he'd been acting with R2-D2, the magic moment didn't seem to mean quite as much to her as it did to him. 'My wife was sitting with a lot of her mates and I go "I worked with R2-D2 today", and they all looked at me and went, "Who?" I guess it's a boy's thing. The chicks just don't get it.'

For much of the filming phase the actors would find themselves acting on partially completed sets, playing against characters and aliens that didn't exist. Much of the background of the movie was to be added in an extensive eighteen-month post-production period, so even the stars found it hard to judge exactly what the movie would be like.

'Now, I've got a real light sabre – imagine that. I've waited twenty years for this moment.'

'On the whole *Star Wars* was a very slow, laborious and exhausting process,' said Ewan, comparing his more character-based roles of the past. 'I mean, it's not like you have to dredge your guts up analysing your character's every thought and whim. I'm playing a hero, a Jedi Knight who has a sense of what's going to happen. Nothing is too much of a surprise for a Jedi.' For a serious-minded actor like Liam Neeson, tackling the role of a venerable Jedi Knight was something of a departure as well. 'The first time Ewan and I had to do any light sabre work, we started making the light sabre noises and soon felt a bit silly,' he admitted during production, after a technician pointed out that the special effects noises would be dubbed on afterwards. 'We kind of looked at each other and had to stop and say, "Wait, we're professional actors here, we can't be doing this!" It's been a bit difficult, acting against things that aren't there.'

Ewan also had other problems with the trademark light sabres. 'The first take and the light sabre literally flew out of my hands,' he admitted sheepishly. 'No-one tells you the sabres have about 10 "D" batteries in them – they burn your hands! I tossed the sabre up in the air and it ended up hitting a technician on the head.'

According to an anonymous friend of Ewan's who spoke to *Film Review*, the actor was finding it hard coping with George Lucas's advanced filming methods, where special effects requirements often took precedence over matters of performance: 'Ewan is as confused as everyone else. Most of what he does is against "blue screen" – he acts against a blank backdrop and the backgrounds and other characters are superimposed later. But he thinks the technology is jaw dropping. It's years ahead of NASA. The thing that impressed him the most was sitting in a chair, being scanned by a computer. Before he knew what was going on there was a realistic, walking, talking copy of him up on the monitors.'

As far as Lucas was concerned, it was largely up to the actors to take care of the acting side of things . 'Lucas is very different, from working on a film with, say, Danny Boyle. With *Star Wars* you shoot a scene and then you take it away and put a load of stuff all over it, do different things to it and change it around – then stick it in the movie. It's a very different process. You could see with George that he's aware of what's "going on" behind you, what's going to be "going on" in front of you and all around you – as well as keeping his eye on what we were doing. Whereas with Danny Boyle, he's only watching us [the actors].'

Naming no names, Ewan claimed, 'There are directors who tell me where to stand, what to say and all that. I mean, they tell me to walk to this point, say the line, and look in that direction. I think "How do they know what I'm going to do?" That type of thing is not why I became an actor.'

Ewan was aware that his perfomances might get lost in among the whizz-bang special effects trickery of *Star Wars*: 'There was eighteen months of post-production, two years of pre-production and three and a half months of shooting. That shows you how important the acting is. I never walked into it expecting to give an Oscar-winning performance, but I think I did a good job and the film will turn out to be absolutely what it was meant to be. I looked at an interview Alec Guinness did when he played Obi-Wan. He said: "My feeling about *Star Wars* is that I delivered the lines and I hope they do the backgrounds nicely." I feel the same way.'

'It's rough because you're not sure about the finished product. That's not satisfying artistically. Then again, those laser sabre battles are like swashbuckling. Every once in a while, I'd be in one of those and suddenly stop and my mind would scream "Aaaah! I'm in *Star Wars*!"

'It's not demanding in terms of emotions, but it was very tiring because of the slow process with special effects. Sci-fi movies are really tough, but I just have a very lazy show in the end.'

Shooting of the film was hit by disaster on 29 July 1997 when the location at Tozeur on the edge of the Sahara Desert in Tunisia was struck by a devastating sand storm.

The cast and crew were in the hotel that evening, enjoying dinner after a day's shooting out in the dunes. As they ate, they were enjoying the spectacular lights above the desert. A series of brilliant bluish white flashes would appear, followed by darkness. The first indication that this was more serious than just a summer-time light show came when additional members of the cast and crew began rushing inside the hotel as the wind picked up and they sought shelter.

Suddenly, it was clear that this was a major storm – one which could have catastrophic consequences for the production. As the wind buffeted the hotel, people were directed to seek shelter in the production offices. A command centre was quickly set up, contacting the location office to order people to evacuate and head back to the hotel as quickly as possible. This meant abandoning expensive camera equipment, hundreds of specially-made props, costumes and countless other items associated with the location.

That night a series of emergency meetings was held to prepare the production for the worst possibility the next day. If the crew were to discover the set had been entirely demolished, it was important that shooting should still continue. The 170-strong crew were only scheduled to film in the desert for ten days and so any delays could be disastrous. Each department head, from props to creature creators, costumes to set builders, was asked to come up with contingency plans to recreate what was needed for the next day's scenes from material that was already safely stored and available in the hotel.

Early the following day a four-wheel-drive production vehicle was sent out to scout the location, long before the sun had risen. The aim was to see if the site still existed and to assess the impact of the damage before other crew members set out from the hotel. After an hour, a radio message was received and producer Rick McCallum assembled another crew to begin the task of rebuilding.

Still in the dark, the convoy arrived with the production crew and cast members – including Liam Neeson and Ewan McGregor – preparing themselves for the worst. The desert was actually wet that morning. The site that greeted them was like the aftermath of a tornado in America's Mid-West. Costumes littered the desert floor as the costuming tents had been blown away. The tents that had been used as dressing rooms for the stars were in shreds. Metal scaffolding which had supported some of the sets was laid bare, twisted and broken. Plaster-built sets had crumbled and landspeeder props had been piled up one on top of another as if some huge collision had taken place between racing speeders. The damage was as bad as McCallum had feared.

Despite this set back, Lucas quickly assembled a crew and devised a way to begin the day's filming, while construction, props and costumes set about retrieving what they could from the mess nature had made. Similarly, Lucas had second unit director Roger Christian get to work just as quickly, working around the destruction that had replaced their carefully constructed location. Rick McCallum got on with co-ordinating the necessary rebuilding.

Shouts in French, Arabic and English filled the air as the production crew got together to save their film from disaster. As Lucas filmed Ewan and Neeson going through their Jedi paces, he couldn't help but reflect that despite all the film-making technology that he was exploiting to bring his vision to the screen, even he was still at the mercy of the power of nature – a truly devastating force.

The site was restored amazingly quickly and less than a day was lost from the schedule. Lucas reflected that this had happened to him before, back in 1976 when he was on the same location, shooting the original *Star Wars*, while for McCallum the experience brought back memories of earthquakes and flooding he'd endured while producing the *Young Indiana Jones* TV series. As for Ewan – he'd never seen anything like it before.

Following location shooting in Italy as well as Tunisia, the film relocated back to Leavesden for the studio-based filming, the end of a fourteen-week space odyssey. This shooting was conducted in amazing secrecy with special electronic passes being issued to cast and crew members. Lucas was adamant that details of the film should not be leaked in advance of the movie's release in 1999, except through official, sanctioned sources. To that end, principal cast and crew members – including Ewan McGregor – had to sign confidentiality agreements.

Left: Ewan with co-star Jane Horrocks who plays the leading female role in Little Voice *and below; Ewan and co-star Christian Bale at the opening of* Velvet Goldmine *at the Edinburgh International Film Festival 1998.*

It was even rumoured that bonus payments had been promised if certain facts didn't leak out. It was also being said that fake script pages, production drawings and story details were being prepared to see where leaks might be coming from. Desperation on the part of the press for scoop stories in the face of this secrecy led to a low-flying helicopter buzzing the backlot at Leavesden – no doubt with a dare-devil photographer hanging out the door hoping to snatch some dramatic pictures. Although a handful of images did leak out, nothing major escaped this security operation and filming wrapped quietly at the end of September 1997.

Traditionally, the completion of principal photography is the end of shooting on a movie for the cast and crew. Post-production, where editing, special effects, sound dubbing and titles are added, follows. For Lucasfilm, this traditional method was old fashioned. George Lucas wanted a more dynamic, open-ended production process. Using new technology to create much of his film, he wanted to be as free as possible to change elements and even change the direction of the storyline if he decided to – or if major plot points should leak out and need altering. That could mean regrouping the principal actors for some further filming work, maybe even more than once.

A source from the set had confirmed this approach: 'So much of what this movie is remains only in George's head at this time and as he has told us, that may really become something different before the film takes its final form.'

So it was that Ewan found himself contractually bound to maintain his distinctive Jedi hair style – which included an extra long section he'd flip back behind one ear – over the Christmas and New Year period of 1997 through into 1998. He was duly back at Leavesden from 18 March 1998, shooting additional material apparently involving the character of Yoda – who was realised in the new film as a combination of traditional puppetry (carried out and voiced by ex-Muppet man and movie director Frank Oz) and computer-generated imagery.

By the summer of 1998, post-production on *The Phantom Menace* had switched to Skywalker Ranch, a production facility owned by George Lucas in Marin County, California. Editing of a rough cut of the movie was underway, while Industrial Light and Magic worked on refining some of the special effects material. By July 1998, a full ten months before the film's planned opening in America, a sizeable chunk of the movie had been screened for representatives of toy licensees who would be marketing the merchandise that tied into the film.

That screening led to a controversy over the nature of Lucas's mystical Force and the possible religious overtones of the film. Some licensees became concerned that the scenes they'd been shown seemed to imply some sort of 'virgin birth' for the boy who was to become Darth Vader, essentially making the villain of the *Star Wars* universe a kind of fallen Christ figure. Worried about the impact this might have in the conservative heartland of the United States, many licensees were reportedly lobbying Lucas to alter this aspect of his story.

The production was hit by another media storm with reports that a full 40 per cent of the footage shot was unusable, due to focusing or filming problems with the new digital cameras. As the hype in advance of release drew closer, so the fan interest and obsession exploded, resulting in rumours like this spilling over the Internet and into print. It fell to Lucasfilm to fully deny the stories, one after another. Other stories claimed Ewan's footage from Tunisia was unusable due to him being visibly ill with tonsillitis – or was it a hangover? – making reshoots inevitable. With a complete curtain of secrecy surrounding the project, it seemed preferable to George Lucas to have wild rumours circulating than to have the real facts leaking out.

Star Wars: The Phantom Menace also attracted more positive publicity for breaking new ground. It was one of the first movies to boast a 24-hour production schedule. Due to massive improvements in the ability to transfer computer data between the UK and California, Lucas could send over digitised dailies from London to Los Angeles where they'd be worked on by ILM while he slept, ready to be reviewed the following day.

With further shooting scheduled for August 1998 – mainly featuring Liam Neeson – the production saga looked unlikely to end for Ewan until the film was finally released. Even the new score for the movie, by composer John Williams, wasn't set to be composed until February 1999, a mere two months before release.

One thing McGregor hadn't given much thought to was the effect the film was likely to have on both his private and professional lives. If he'd thought the fuss surrounding *Trainspotting* had been extreme, the feeding frenzy that was bound to descend on him in May 1999 was going to be something else. But he felt secure enough in his own career to realise that *Star Wars* –

professionally – was just one job among the others, no matter how extraordinary the production process or audience reaction. It was not always thus. 'I knew it was going to be enormous when it came out,' said Ewan, 'and I've never been in anything like that before. I wondered how it would juxtapose with the other work I was doing. Some of the actors in the original Star Wars didn't do anything else afterwards, and I wondered, is that going to happen to me?'

With the potential to become the new Harrison Ford, Ewan McGregor – self-deprecating as ever – had another perspective on his possible future. On his TV interview with Michael Parkinson, he reflected: 'Look what happened to Mark Hamill!'

Despite having to be available throughout 1998 for any further additional shooting on *Star Wars: The Phantom Menace*, Ewan wasn't about to stop making movies. 'His roles in *Little Voice*, *Rogue Trader*, *Eye of the Beholder* and *Nora* were all in the can before his 1998 return to the stage in *Little Malcolm and his Struggle Against the Eunuchs*. By the end of the year, though, he would be having second thoughts about the pace of his movie-making and the price of fame.

Such was Ewan's growing fame that he was one of the first men to be featured on the Pirelli calendar, a favourite of garage mechanics everywhere. 'None of the men are nude' said Pirelli spokeswoman Lisa Needham of Ewan's debut in the 1998 calendar, tucked up in bed with only his head showing. 'They are simply portraits of famous gentlemen. It's very tasteful.'

'When I first met R2-D2 I almost went down on the ground. My wife was sitting with a lot of her mates and I go "I worked with R2-D2 today", and they all looked at me and went, "Who?" I guess it's a boy's thing. The chicks just don't get it.'

During production of *Star Wars* that previous summer, Ewan had the cover of America's popular showbusiness bible *Entertainment Weekly* devoted to him. However, Ewan would not be following his *Trainspotting* co-star Johnny Lee Miller to 'valium haze LA'. 'Look at Minnie Driver,' he accusingly spoke of Matt Damon's English co-star in his self-penned Oscar winner *Good Will Hunting*, in a remark he would later regret. 'She's completely re-invented herself – she's gone mad. Why has she bothered buying into all that rubbish?'.

Ewan continued to insist that if a film-maker wanted him for a role, provision must be made for his wife and daughter to accompany him to the location. 'I don't care if people find it unusual, or what people think at all,' he said of the familial arrangement. 'I think it's only good, we're happy, we can travel around together . . . you're building up a future together. People are so sceptical and I think that makes it all the stronger.'

While his approach to the work hadn't changed, Ewan had had to adopt to newfound celebrity and success. After *Trainspotting*, he was hailed as the biggest thing to come out of Scotland since ex-Bond star Sean Connery. (In some circles, he was even being talked of as a potential future Bond.) 'I'm from Scotland and most people are very narrow minded about things', said Ewan of the facile comparison. 'So, they go "Scotland – Sean Connery – he was an actor, too! You're an actor, so you're the new Sean Connery!" Right.'

McGregor claimed that celebrity hadn't changed him. Despite his workload, his family were still more important than fame and fortune. 'You know, I've only been in Cannes once, with *Trainspotting*. I was with my wife and kid coming back and reading something like *Hello* or *Tatler* or some shite, saying, "Oh, Ewan McGregor is there with his fashion accessory wife and child." My fashion accessory wife and baby? Please! That's disgusting, actually.'

Despite his protestations about the downside of fame, he did have a big house in London and the security of money in the bank. However, an ostentatious lifestyle just wasn't for him. Ewan is still too much of a middle-class Calvinist kid at heart, who believes he has to work to earn his living. 'I'm putting it away,' is all he would say of the money he was making.

He also kept largely quiet about the time and money he devoted to charities, in particular Marie Curie Cancer Care, and the Rachel House Children's Hospice in Fife. He had developed an understanding of coping with ill and dying children after his experience with Clara's meningitis, and had visited Rachel House to find out more about its work in February 1998. 'As

'Denis helped me with my audition speeches when I started out. I've been watching him perform all my life.'

a parent I can appreciate how terrible it is when your child gets sick,' he said after the visit, 'but these parents have to deal with children who continue being sick. They're all amazing.'

From the big-budget, out-of-this-world adventure of *Star Wars*, Ewan came spinning back down to earth with a bump – landing at the fading English seaside resort of Scarborough for *Little Voice*.

Originally a stage play written by Jim Cartwright, *Little Voice* centres around a terribly shy girl named Laura Hoff – played by Jane Horrocks, who featured with Ewan in the *Tales from the Crypt* episode 'The Cold War' – who rises to fame due to her almost supernatural ability to mimic the singing voices of Shirley Bassey and Judy Garland.

When American film company Miramax bought the film rights to the play after a hectic bidding war, it was claimed they wanted to Americanise the story and turn it into a vehicle for Gwyneth Paltrow – then more famous for being the girlfriend of Brad Pitt than for her later roles in *Sliding Doors* or *Shakespeare in Love*. However, director Mark Herman, who had last worked with Ewan on *Brassed Off*, felt it was unthinkable to do *Little Voice* without Horrocks in the leading role of Laura.

'Those laser sabre battles are like swashbuckling. Every once in a while, I'd be in one of those and suddenly stop and my mind would scream "Aaagh! I'm in Star Wars!".'

McGregor was brought in to play Billy, an anti-social pigeon fancier and potential boyfriend for Laura. The utterly unglamorous role was a return to his acting roots – just raw performance, no special effects, aliens or computerised backdrops. It was a galaxy far, far away from *Star Wars*.

Also in the cast was veteran British actor Michael Caine, one of the few Hollywood superstars Britain has produced, in the role of a talent scout. Caine saw a bright future ahead for McGregor: 'I think he's a major talent. Movie acting is deceptively simple – the reason is, if you do it right it looks simple, but it's very difficult to do it right. Ewan does – he'll go right to the top.'

Whilst filming in the northern English town of Scarborough, during September through November 1997, director Herman saw how the actor reacted when faced with his fans. 'You notice it when you're out with him. It takes a few minutes, and then word spreads and crowds gather. Some actors would just get out of there, but he's very generous with the time he gives to the public.'

There were even surprises in store for Ewan in the town's night-clubs. 'The first night I went out to a club, the DJ put on the *Trainspotting* track with my "Choose life" dialogue on it and I'd never heard it before. There I was dancing at the time.'

Little Voice proved popular as the opening film of the 1998 London Film Festival, before going on to a wider release in the UK and United States. *Variety* called the film 'a small picture with a big heart . . . smooth direction and juicy performances by a host of Brit character actors ensure an entertaining ride'. The only real note of criticism came for those parts of the film featuring McGregor's character, described as 'a romantic subplot that plays like an after-thought'.

During the making of *Little Voice*, Ewan was approached about a role in another low-budget British film. This was based on the real-life downfall of a stock market trader. Ewan was ready to say no, until he discovered it was the story of disgraced Barings Bank trader Nick Leeson. 'I thought a film about traders must be very dull,' he said, 'but in fact it's an incredible story and not the kind of part that I've played before, so it's good.'

Rogue Trader originated with a television interview between David Frost and Leeson, then imprisoned in Frankfurt prior to extradition to Singapore for his involvement in the 1995 collapse of Barings Bank. Frost was fascinated by Leeson's story and bought the rights to his autobiography, written in prison.

Frost recruited British film-maker James Dearden as screenwriter/director, and Paul Raphael as the film's producer. 'Ewan McGregor is the one young British star who's perfect for the part,' claimed Raphael, adding that 'he could get the film financed,' and that it was the kind of role which Gary Oldman would once have played. This was not the first time Ewan had been compared to Oldman, a British ex-pat who had conquered a drinking problem. When asked which British actors he admires, however, Ewan rarely mentions stateside success stories Oldman and Tim Roth. Instead, he names Ian Hart, best known for Ken Loach's polemical film *Land and Freedom*. (Admiring Roth for sticking to his principles [that's because he only does good work], McGregor is more scathing about Oldman. 'He's survived the crap, but only up to a point.')

Filming began on *Rogue Trader* in November 1997, with McGregor going straight from *Little Voice* to Richmond Park in south-west London to shoot a wedding scene. Production then switched to Gatwick for airport scenes, including a recreation of the famous news footage of Leeson being escorted through the airport by the police. Filming continued in London until Christmas 1997, before wrapping in January 1998 with location shooting in Malaysia and Singapore.

In preparing for *Rogue Trader*, there was little chance to get close to the real Nick Leeson. 'He's banged up in Singapore and I couldn't get in there, I don't think,' said Ewan. 'And I don't want to meet him, because I don't want to know what he's like too much. I don't want to have any opinion about him, because people are very black-and-white about the case. Some people think he's a complete animal and some people think that he's a victim. I want to play it in the middle.'

Paul Raphael was equally insistent that the film would neither whitewash or crucify Leeson. 'He's not a saint in our film,' he said of Ewan's characterisation, 'but he's not an evil guy, either. He's not the only person who ever acted irresponsibly in the banking sector, but he lost control, got caught and ended up with a pretty rough deal – six years in jail. People were happy to turn a blind eye while the profits rolled in . . .'

McGregor and director Deardon were worried about the film glamorising Leeson's financial misadventures, but Dearden felt Ewan hit the right note in his performance. 'Ewan McGregor looks like a slob in the film. But Ewan has a lot of charm – and so did Nick. He could be seductive when he wanted to be.'

Back in Britain during the studio work at Pinewood, stories emerged from the set concerning a supposed relationship between Ewan and co-star Anna Friel. Cast opposite Ewan as Leeson's wife, the young actress was formerly best known for her controversial lesbian role on the British TV soap opera *Brookside*. As soon as the stories hit the press, Friel was quick to pour cold water on them while praising her co-star to the skies.

Pictures of the pair kissing – taken during romantic scenes between Leeson and his wife-to-be, Lisa, filmed in Malaysia – hit the press, giving a distorted view of the actors' relationship. 'There was a great chemistry between us,' Friel admitted. 'It's amazing – we are from exactly the same background and had exactly the same views and opinions. If I could be a female version of anybody, I think it would be him. So, of course, people said there must be a relationship. Think what you want – but we know.'

Despite echoes of the Cameron Diaz allegations, Ewan kept quiet. He was more concerned with Eve, Clara and *Rogue Trader* than responding to the latest British press rumours. 'The hard thing about success,' he said, 'is that work starts to demand all your time and that's not good for any relationship. One of the reasons I took the summer of 1998 off was to spend more time with Eve. She's very down to earth with it, as I am. She knows who I am completely. She knows I'm a scallywag, but not one who's gonna fuck around with her.'

For her part, Eve was getting used to exploitative press coverage of their private lives. 'Ewan is very close to his family and I am very close to my family,' she told *Vanity Fair*. 'We have the same values, but it's quite pernicious the way it hits you. The papers always say, "Oh, Ewan, he's so nice, so grounded," but, I mean, Ewan is a nice guy, so even if he's not grounded, he's going to be nice . . . [the press] have ways to hurt people. I'm not sure of it yet, I'm still watching.'

Shooting at London's Pinewood studios, where the SIMEX trading floor from Singapore was recreated, allowed Ewan to stay at home with his family in the evenings after filming. Amid the studio hustle and bustle, clad in a blue-and-yellow-striped jacket, Ewan practised hand signals used by stock traders the world over while cradling at least two telephones. 'This jacket is based upon Nick Leeson's trading jacket,' he explained of his attire. 'It's exactly as it would have been. The tie, though, actually was Nick Leeson's. I got it from one of his friends – it's a Gucci tie. His friend Danny said he never made a penny while wearing this tie, so he stopped wearing it to work.'

The film wrapped in January 1998 and Ewan moved on to his next project. There was a shock in store for the film-makers, however, when in August 1998 it was announced that Leeson was suffering from cancer, had undergone an operation and could either be transferred to the UK or even released from prison early. McGregor courted controversy by joining calls for Leeson to serve time in the UK, instead of Singapore's Changi Prison. 'I made a comment that he should be allowed to come back to England because he's got cancer. The Foreign Office rang up my agent and said: "If Ewan McGregor wants to bring Leeson back, he should do it through us and not the media." So that's fine, then.'

Rogue Trader would not see the light of day in the UK until 1999, alongside the equally delayed *Nightwatch* and *The Serpent's Kiss*. McGregor became conscious that the delays made it seem as if every other film that was opening starred him. 'I keep saying I'm not going to work for two months. Then somebody says, "What about this?" and I go, "Oh, okay." I've got to say "no", but I'm just not very good at that. You make a bunch of movies and they release them all at once, so you look like you're working like a madman.'

He didn't say no to *Eye of the Beholder* either – a psychological thriller directed by Stephan Elliot, who made camp comedy-drama *The Adventures of Priscilla, Queen of the Desert*, which featured Terence Stamp (also to be seen in the *Star Wars* prequel) in a dress. Shooting began in Montreal at the end of March 1998, after a short break at home with the family following the completion of *Rogue Trader*, and re-shoots for *Star Wars*.

Based on the cult novel by Marc Behm, *Eye of the Beholder* is the story of a disillusioned surveillance detective (Ewan) who becomes obsessed with a mysterious woman (Ashley Judd), who leads him on a ten-year odyssey. He shadows the woman, a serial killer of men, without her ever knowing, at times even protecting her from the consequences of her actions.

Moving rapidly from one film to another, Ewan tackled each character as a new challenge as with his roles in *Emma,* and, to an extent, *Nightwatch*. 'There's a point, about two weeks before you shoot, where you think, maybe this is the role I won't be able to crack,' he admitted, 'but the pace keeps you well-oiled, too.'

'Well-oiled' might have been the condition Ewan was in when, during a break from shooting *Eye of the Beholder*, he attended a World Cup party in Paris before the Scotland versus Brazil opening match in June 1998. The party, at the Buddha Bar, was packed with Scottish celebrities showing support for their soon-to-be-defeated side. As the Scottish band Cullin Music took to the stage, Sean Connery called for the crowd to get up and dance. In the next instance Connery was up on the stage, closely followed by Ewan.

As more Scottish celebrities crowded the stage — among them racing-driver Jackie Stewart, footballers Kenny Dalglish and Ally McCoist, chat show host Fred MacAulay, comic actor Richard Wilson and Scottish National Party leader Alex Salmond — things became a bit unstable. 'It got to the point where our keyboard player, Kirsten, had to bodily push Sean off her instruments, and Ewan McGregor knelt down and held the equipment steady to avoid a disaster,' band member Martyn Bennett recalled.

Also at this time, Ewan appeared on MacAulay's BBC1 chat show, broadcast from Paris. Despite the presence of mother Carol and father Jim, he was clearly the worse for drink, and the interview quickly descended into an innuendo-laden farce.

Although drinking never seemed to interfere with his professionalism, the role of the professional drunk was clearly one which Ewan loved to play up to. 'It's just a state of being for me, I'm usually drunk,' he gleefully announced to *The Face* during a promotional interview for *A Life Less Ordinary*. 'It's no big story with me anymore. I've yet to be found in a gutter somewhere. I always get away with it somehow.'

However, so many people commented on McGregor's drinking that he began to take it a little more seriously. 'There was a time when I drank to deal with all the stress of work,' he finally admitted. 'But that's the road to ruin, so I decided to sort things out.' His decision to address his drinking was in response to concerns Eve had expressed privately, and had tentatively hinted at in the few interviews she had given.

The incident in Paris was not the first time Ewan turned a TV appearance into a fiasco. In 1996, he was one of several guests on Chris Evans' live show *TFI Friday* whose on-the-air-swearing brought complaints from the public. The Independent Television Commission upheld the complaints and, consequently, the show had to be pre-recorded and edited before transmission from there onward.

Ewan, who found it difficult to tone down his language in interviews, was to discover that profanity was not as acceptable in print, or on radio or TV, as it was on film. One particular interview in *The Face* made him conscious of the habit, 'I like swearing,' he claimed, 'but I was really embarrassed. My dad was phoning and saying, "Ewan, you've got to stop swearing when you're doing interviews." I said, "Oh, I'm sorry, I'm sorry." You forget that they're sitting up there in Scotland and all their friends are reading it. All my teachers . . .' Jim McGregor was particularly upset because the headmaster of Morrison's Academy read the offending article.

After the World Cup trip, Ewan, Eve and Clara took a more low-key family holiday in France. However, two events from around this time would come back to haunt him in subsequent months.

In September, McGregor made off-the-cuff but ill-advised comments at the Deauville Film Festival in France, where he was serving on the jury. Asked about his favourite actors, journalists

noted how the rising star didn't mention Connery, despite their seemingly cordial relations during the World Cup. It became clear that this meeting of Scottish film stars had not been a meeting of minds – at least politically. 'Being Scottish is not the same for me as it is for Sean Connery,' explained McGregor, who had endured Connery lecturing him in Paris about the SNP and independence. 'I don't like to be told by anyone how to feel about being Scottish. Nobody has the right to tell me – especially somebody who hasn't lived there for 25 years.'

The direct dig at Connery's self-imposed tax exile status caused controversy in the Scottish press – so much so that within a month, McGregor was backtracking from his remarks during a visit to Edinburgh's Butterfly World with some of the families and patients of the children's hospice Rachel House. 'I want to make it clear that we are not in any argument,' he told the assembled press. 'I will not be held up as some kind of figurehead against the independence of Scotland because, quite frankly, that's not true.'

> 'The script is all that's important to me. I go with my gut instinct having read a script. That's the only thing that informs my choice.'

This wasn't enough for some of the Scottish press, with the *Daily Record*, dismissing his apology as half-hearted gibberish. Later, Ewan denied there had ever been a significant rift between him and Connery, seeing the whole incident as a media-invented fiction. 'I love his acting, I never had a fight with him. Complete nonsense. I said that I didn't like him preaching at me because my politics are private, but the Scottish press turned it into a Ewan v Sean battle over independence, which was a good story. I don't live there, so I don't want to pontificate about it, but I'm very proud about being Scottish and I'm not anti-independence.'

As a result of the controversy, Ewan had a conciliatory meeting with SNP leader Alex Salmond to discuss his views on Scottish independence, and a rather awkward telephone conversation with Connery in the hope of smoothing-over ruffled feathers.

In 1999 Ewan hoped to play Irish writer James Joyce in *Nora*, named after Joyce's mistreated wife Nora (to be played by Susan Lynch). The attraction for Ewan – who had long been attached to the project in a production, as well as an acting capacity – was to capture 'the true nastiness of the man' regarded as one of the world's most impenetrable novelists, and also one of the greatest. (Ewan himself never managed to finish reading Joyce's *Ulysses*.)

While in Canada filming *Eye of the Beholder*, McGregor discovered that *Nora* was not to go into production in mid-1998 as expected. 'I heard that we had lost out on funding to make *Nora*. I was in a bad state, exhausted and depressed. Looking back, I got lower than I ever could have imagined.'

Despite the set-back, the film secured financing and was rescheduled for shooting, barring any further cancellations, in Dublin and Trieste, March 1999. 'It's more about his relationship with his wife than his books,' Ewan has said, 'and that relationship was all over the place. It was very sexual and passionate one minute, and so cold, so mean the next. It's a really dirty, sexy script.'

One of the attractions of *Nora* was the chance to work with a female director, Pat Murphy. 'It's really peculiar I haven't worked with a woman after all the films I've done,' mused Ewan.

Rumours of one other project proved surprising even for McGregor. 'I was glad to read in the newspapers that I might be playing John Lennon. That would be very nice, but I don't know anything about it. Yoko never got through. Maybe she left a message and I never got it. "Yoko, dahhling! Of course I will!" But I'd have to think about that one, because none of the other Beatles would want her to make the film, so I probably wouldn't do it.'

Despite his stated lack of directorial ambitions, Ewan McGregor began to plan his behind-the-camera debut in November 1998. In a cruelly funny short film called *Desserts*, supporting the British comedy *Divorcing Jack*, Ewan starred as a 'Stroller' who discovers an untouched chocolate eclair on a deserted beach. After gingerly testing the cream, Ewan proceeds to stuff the eclair into his mouth, only for the tables to be turned and the character to get his 'just desserts'.

It was the black humour of the piece, and the minimal commitment required, which saw Ewan make his third short film appearance, this time for writer-director Jeff Stark. 'I was faxed the script – and it was just one sheet of paper, but it made me laugh so much that I just had to do it,' said Ewan. 'We shot for one day on the West coast of Scotland and it's quite an interesting piece of work.'

It was to the short form which Ewan himself turned when offered the chance to direct a segment of *Tube Tales*, a compendium film funded by Sky Movies recounting ten tales of true-life experiences on the London Underground. (Other directors included Ewan's pal Jude Law, Pulp front man Jarvis Cocker and satirist Armando Iannucci.) Ewan's nine-minute sequence concentrated on a young couple who find romance on the Underground, only for it to go spectacularly wrong. The film also saw a reunion between McGregor and *Trainspotting/Shallow Grave* director of photography Brian Tufano.

With *Nora* postponed, Ewan found a hole in his schedule which allowed him to work with his uncle and early inspiration, Denis Lawson. Although primarily interested in film acting, Ewan had in recent years harboured an ambition to return to the stage, following his one and only professional stage experience playing Nick in Joe Orton's *What The Butler Saw*, early in 1993.

The idea for a return to the stage had occurred in a phone call between Ewan and Lawson during the shooting of *A Life Less Ordinary*. Ewan knew there would be big risks involved in him taking to the boards again: 'It's a dangerous thing for me to contemplate right now. With the British love of building someone up and then tearing them down, I'm setting myself up for some serious abuse.' But he had powerful reasons for returning to live performing. 'I really miss the whole process of rehearsing with a bunch of people, and that paralysing fear of the first night and the adrenaline rush that comes afterwards.'

To avoid major embarrassment, Ewan and his uncle, who they intended to direct, opted to keep the production small and intimate. 'I won't be doing *Hamlet* at the National,' Ewan said, perhaps alluding to fellow film thespian Keanu Reeves' stint as the Prince in Winnipeg, Canada, in 1994. Having recruited a couple of friends Ewan was keen to work with, he and Lawson began to look for a suitable play. 'If I do it on my own terms, I stand a better chance of surviving the experience,' he reflected.

Eventually they chose David Halliwell's 1960's political satire, *Little Malcolm and His Struggle Against the Eunuchs*, which was made into a movie in 1974, with John Hurt and David Warner, under the abbreviated title *Little Malcolm*. Those who knew McGregor felt he could only benefit from this break from his celluloid career. *Brassed Off / Little Voice* director Mark Herman opined: 'Ewan knew he'd been doing too much, too quickly. He was a bit frazzled. This will probably be good for him.'

Their plans quickly came to fruition. Previews ran at the Hampstead Theatre from 12 November 1998, followed by the opening night on 18 November. The full run sold out within days, with black market tickets changing hands for up to £200 each. When he heard of the inflated prices, Ewan volunteered to man a telephone on the theatre's jammed switchboard.

Coincidentally, Ewan became the latest in a line of movie stars who had taken to the London stage, including Ralph Fiennes, Kevin Spacey, Juliette Binoche and Nicole Kidman. *Little Malcolm*, however, was a true McGregor family event, with Lou Gish, daughter of Lawson's partner Sheila Gish, joining the cast and the whole family, including Ewan's grandmother Phyllis, attending the first night.

Ewan portrayed rebellious student Malcolm Scrawdyke for the princely sum of only £250 per week. 'It's a rather cruel comedy about a student who's suspended from art school for being a disruptive influence,' explained Ewan. 'He goes off to plot his revenge against the world and, together with three friends, forms the Party of Dynamic Erection in his ice-cold studio.'

There was no wild party after the first night – Ewan, Denis and the family enjoyed a quiet meal at a nearby restaurant. The good reviews that Ewan received the following morning led very quickly to speculation about a West End transfer, or a film adaptation of the play.

Nicholas de Jongh, writing in the *Evening Standard*, claimed Ewan 'loses neither his charisma nor his personality on stage', *The Times* said that Ewan's 'escape from screen to stage was well worth it', while in *The Guardian* theatre critic Michael Billington noted that although Ewan was 'cast against type, he acquits himself extremely well in Denis Lawson's swift, sharply edited revival . . . he gives a commanding performance that proves conclusively that McGregor can hold a stage.' *The Sun* advised its readers – not known for theatre-going – to 'kill for tickets!' The *Daily Telegraph* called his performance 'terrific', while the *Mirror* stated that 'McGregor gives a mesmeric performance' and played the leading role 'with great conviction'. It was the *Daily Mail* which summed up the collective view: 'Ewan McGregor returns to the stage in triumph.'

Following this triumph at the theatre, Ewan was free to enjoy a quiet Christmas with his family, before the hysteria of the new *Star Wars* release in 1999.

'I've always wanted to go to Hollywood, drive big cars and be in big movies,' Ewan once joked, while dismissing any suggestion of becoming a Beverly Hills recluse. 'I stayed at the Mondrian [exclusive Hollywood hotel] once. God! All these snotty wee guys in suits came running out to the driveway and told my cab to move on. Then when they realised I was actually staying there, they're all "Oh, sorry, sir, please let us help you . . ." They said to me, "Well, obviously you're familiar with the Sky bar." I said, "No, never heard of it," and they all started laughing: "Oh! My Gad! Can you believe it, he's never heard of the Sky bar!"'

As the 21st century loomed, Ewan could pick and choose his roles. Committed to featuring as Obi Wan Kenobi in two further *Star Wars* prequels, in the years 2000 and 2002 respectively, there would be plenty of time in between for other projects.

Scottish screenwriter/director/actor David Hayman nurtured long term plans for a film in which McGregor would play Robert Burns. Producer Richard Scott-Thompson linked Ewan's name to a prospective film on the life of Thomas Blake Glover, a Scottish-born nineteenth-century samurai who helped defeat the Shogun empire and founded the Mitsubishi company. (Glover was also famous for an affair with a Japanese woman which inspired the opera *Madame Butterfly* and – a sure attraction to Ewan – for having his face on the label for bottled Kirin Beer.) Scott-Thompson predicted that, 'Ideally, we could have Ewan McGregor as the young Glover and Sean Connery as the older Glover,' estimating that the project would take two years to complete.

Also on the cards was a possible film project with Denis Lawson. The tale of a struggling Scottish rock band, *Don't Think Twice*, was scheduled for shooting in the west of Scotland after they completed their theatre run of *Little Malcolm*. In the midst of all this, Ewan found time to join forces with Bridget Fonda for an action-film-cum-love-story entitled *South From Hell's Kitchen*.

In addition, Ewan still found time for personal projects of his own. Back in 1995, along with actors Jude Law, Law's actress wife Sadie Frost and former co-star Johnny Lee Miller (from *Trainspotting*) and Sean Pertwee (from *Blue Juice*), Ewan formed a production company with the name Natural Nylon (Nylon derived from New York and London). It would enable the actors to make their own films while staying outside of the Hollywood system. All five had agreed to feature in *The Hellfire Club*, an £8-million movie about England's eighteenth-century secret society, with Ewan as corrupt politician John Wilkes. McGregor also planned to produce his James Joyce project *Nora* through Natural Nylon early in 1999. With $100 million in finance, they had the resources to produce ten films in Britain over the next five years.

Other potential Natural Nylon projects include a film about Elizabethan playwright Christopher Marlowe, an adaptation of Iain Banks' novel *The Bridge* and Christopher Fowler's *Psychoville*. Ewan himself was also said to be interested in the lead for the film of Iain Banks' contemporary thriller *Complicity* – indeed, the character in the book could have been modelled on his journalist in *Shallow Grave* – though it seemed more likely Johnny Lee Miller would win the part. All would have to wait, however, until Natural Nylon finished working on David Cronenberg's futuristic thriller *Existenz*, set in the world of virtual reality games.

Whichever of these diverse projects came to the screen, there was one film which would have nothing to do with Ewan McGregor. Andrew Macdonald had snapped up the rights to the Alex Garland best-seller *The Beach*, commissioning a screenplay from partner John Hodge, with last member of the triumvirate Danny Boyle slated to direct.

The only person missing from the *Shallow Grave/Trainspotting/A Life Less Ordinary* team was Ewan. Informal discussions had indicated he was bound to get the role, so it came as something of a shock when Leonardo DiCaprio was announced as the lead at a fee of around $20 million.

'I was very surprised that they chose Leonardo over me,' admitted a clearly fazed Ewan in August 1998. 'It was down to money. Danny can get a bigger budget with him. To be a part of that team is very important to me. I thought we were more than that.' As far as Ewan had come, the commercial failure of *A Life Less Ordinary* had not granted him any extra potency at the American box office. But still, he had stuck with Hodge, Macdonald and Boyle, when it would have been relatively easy to take high-profile, high-paying Hollywood movies.

'Success in America seems to be their goal at the moment,' said Ewan of his three erstwhile pals. 'It never was our goal before, so I don't understand why it's suddenly the mission. I didn't think that was the point . . . I was gutted. Fucking gutted . . . It's been kind of like a love affair between Danny and me – and now he's seeing someone else.'

When Ewan was subsequently asked to step into a role vacated by Leonardo – that of anti-hero Patrick Bateman in the film version of Brett Easton Ellis's controversial novel *American Psycho* – he declined. It left the way clear for *Velvet Goldmine* co-star Christian Bale to step back into a part which had been his before DiCaprio expressed interest.

At the end of the nineties, Ewan began to feel a critical backlash was inevitable. It seemed impossible to enjoy such good luck and success without the same elements of the press which had raised his media profile turning against him. 'I'll be prick of the year,' he anticipated. 'That's what happens in our country. They build you up, then slag you off.'

For the time being, at least, this was merely the paranoia of a man standing at the top of the heap. When Ewan made the cover of American celebrity magazine *Details*, editor David Keeps wrote as a fan: 'He has this rock star quality. A lot of actors don't – they may be very good or very funny, but he has a quality in his life and in his work that has a kind of rock'n'roll sensibility.'

Ewan himself blanched at this unwanted icon-of-his-generation status: 'I don't stand for anything,' he protested. 'I don't see myself as a figurehead.' Although his rise coincided with an upswing in the fortunes of the British film industry, Ewan saw himself as simply the most visible product of that boom, remembering, with ironic relish, what *Young Americans/Judge Dredd* director Danny Cannon prophesied several years before. 'He sat there and there was me, Sadie Frost and a lot of young British talent who'd just started off', recalled Ewan, 'and he basically told us that we were all wasting our time, that there's nothing good that came out of this country, that if you want to do anything you have to go to the States. Two years later, *Shallow Grave* came out . . .'

Ewan realised he owed his success to the late nineties renaissance in British film. At the same time, he was the actor most empowered to ensure it continued. 'All this didn't happen on its own,' he acknowledged. 'It happened because of the people who are doing it, people who were hungry enough and ballsy enough to make it happen and not take no for an answer.'

At the same time, McGregor had begun to consider the pace of his personal career, and to give some thought to longevity. 'As soon as I started acting professionally,' he reflected, 'it felt like my life had gone into widescreen. That's how it's been ever since. I am exhausted. I've had enough. I have become tainted with the whole thing. I've pushed my career as far as I could, made as many films in a short space of time, but it has become totally mad, just mad.'

This temporary change in priorities allowed Ewan the time to take the title role of *Little Malcolm* at the Hampstead Theatre. As unqualified a success as this was, it seemed but a quiet prelude to the frenzy surrounding the release of *Star Wars Episode 1: The Phantom Menace* in May 1999. When a two-minute trailer for the film was released in November 1998, fans queued round the block and paid $8 a ticket for the privilege, leaving when the main feature began. Featuring snippets of McGregor as Obi Wan Kenobi, the Jedi Knight, the trailer was also released on the Internet, clogging up the *Star Wars* site as fans tried to download a glimpse of the new movie.

Ardent *Star Wars* fans were desperate to get their hands on anything bearing McGregor's/ Kenobi's image, from commemorative Coca Cola cans to pirate photographs of models for the new range of *Star Wars* action figures. If Ewan was about to be troubled by his exploding fame, then his mother was more bothered by the likeness on his action figure: 'I wouldn't recognise my son from the way the doll looks,' said Carol. 'It doesn't really look like Ewan.'

From junkie to Jedi, it has been quite a ride for the boy from Crieff. Balancing low-budget British films with a blockbusting American intergalactic franchise seems like a career strategy which could serve Ewan McGregor well into the 21st century. At its most basic, though, his driven nature is simple – arising from a need to structure his life around his remarkable talent, and to enjoy every last minute of it. 'I have a beautiful wife, and a beautiful child, and fantastic, wonderful parents and I love my job. In fact I'm Mr Fucking Lucky.'

Financially, if Ewan didn't relish the challenge that acting presents, he need never work again. His agent, Lindy King, noted the exponential growth of her client's income over several years. 'For *Trainspotting* Ewan got next to nothing,' she claimed. 'For *Velvet Goldmine* he got ten times that. And for *Star Wars* – well, he'll get ten times that again.' Still, she acknowledged, McGregor is not just working for the money. 'Ewan wants to grow as an actor. Actors don't really do repertory theatre any more – so Ewan has been using the last couple of years as his own repertory experience on screen.'

Ewan McGregor may have an inkling of what the future holds, but its uncertainties still inspire him. 'With *Star Wars* my life is about to go into Super 70mm, but my feelings about it are still the same,' he says. 'It's a different part, a different character – and until it comes out I never know whether I've pulled it off. That's always exciting and also incredibly scary.'

'I don't know what it is with me and cameras,' he concedes, with his customary optimism, 'but whatever it is, I'm bloody glad I've got it!'

FILMOGRAPHY

Being Human USA 1993. 89 minutes. Director: Bill Forsyth. Screenplay: Bill Forsyth. Production Company: Warner Brothers. Cast: Robin Williams (Hector), Robert Carlyle (Prehistoric Shaman) Ewan McGregor (Alvarez)

Shallow Grave USA 1994. 93 minutes. Director: Danny Boyle. Screenplay: John Hodge. Production Companies: Channel Four Films/Figment Films/Glasgow Film Fund/Gramercy Pictures/PolyGram Filmed Entertainment. Cast: Kerry Fox (Juliet Miller), Christopher Eccleston (David Stephens), Ewan McGregor (Alex Law)

Blue Juice UK 1995. 90 minutes. Director: Carl Prechezer. Screenplay: Carl Prechezer, Peter Salmi, Tim Veglio. Production Company: Skreba Films. Cast: Sean Pertwee (JC), Catherine Zeta-Jones (Chloe), Ewan McGregor (Dean Raymond)

The Pillow Book France/UK/Netherlands 1995. 120 minutes. Director: Peter Greenaway. Screenplay: Peter Greenaway. Production Companies: Channel Four Films/Eurimages Fund of the Council of Europe/Alpha Films/Le Studio Canal+/Delux Productions/Kasander & Wigman Productions/Nederlands Fonds voor de Film/Woodline Films. Cast: Vivian Wu (Nagiko), Ewan McGregor (Jerome)

Trainspotting UK 1996. 93 minutes. Director: Danny Boyle. Screenplay: John Hodge, based on the novel by Irvine Welsh. Production Company: Channel Four Films/Figment Films/PolyGram Filmed Entertainment/The Noel Gay Motion Picture Company. Cast: Ewan McGregor (Mark "Rents" Renton), Ewen Bremner (Daniel "Spud" Murphy), Jonny Lee Miller (Simon David "Sick Boy" Williamson), Kevin McKidd (Tommy), Robert Carlyle (Francis "Franco" Begbie), Kelly MacDonald (Diane)

Emma UK/USA 1996. 120 minutes. Director: Douglas McGrath. Screenplay: Douglas McGrath, based on the novel by Jane Austen. Production Company: Haft Entertainment/Matchmaker Films/Miramax Films. Cast: Gwyneth Paltrow (Emma Woodhouse), Greta Scacchi (Mrs. Weston), Jeremy Northam (Mr. Knightley), Ewan McGregor (Frank Churchill)

Nightwatch USA 1996. 101 minutes. Director: Ole Bornedal. Screenplay: Steven Soderbergh based upon the original screenplay for Nattevagten by Ole Bornedal. Production Company: Michael Obel Productions/Dimension Films. Cast: Ewan McGregor (Martin Belos), Nick Nolte (Inspector Thomas Cray), Patricia Arquette (Katherine)

Brassed Off UK/USA 1996. 105 minutes. Director: Mark Herman. Screenplay: Mark Herman. Production Company: Channel Four Films/Miramax Films. Cast: Pete Postlethwaite (Danny), Tara Fitzgerald (Gloria), Ewan McGregor (Andy)

The Serpent's Kiss/ AKA Le Baiser du Serpent France/Germany/UK 1997. 104 minutes. Director: Philippe Rousselot. Screenplay: Tim Rose Price. Production Company: Le Studio Canal+/France 2 Cinéma/Président

Films/Trinity/Berryer Films/Nef/Red Parrot/Rose Price Battsek Productions. Cast: Ewan McGregor (Meneer Chrome), Greta Scacchi (Juliana), Pete Postlethwaite (Thomas Smithers), Carmen Chaplin (Thea)

A Life Less Ordinary UK 1997. 103 minutes. Director: Danny Boyle. Screenplay: John Hodge. Production Company: Figment Films/PolyGram Filmed Entertainment/Channel Four Films. Cast: Cameron Diaz (Celine), Ewan McGregor (Robert), Holly Hunter (O'Reilly)

Velvet Goldmine UK/USA 1997. 124 minutes. Director: Todd Haynes. Screenplay: Todd Haynes, story by Todd Haynes and James Lyons. Production Company: Channel Four Films/Miramax Films/Zenith/Single Cell Pictures/Killer Films/Goldwyn Films/Newmarket Capital Group. Cast: Ewan McGregor (Curt Wild), Christian Bale (Arthur Stuart), Eddie Izzard (Jerry Divine),

Star Wars: Episode One USA 1998. 120 minutes. Director: George Lucas. Screenplay: George Lucas. Production Company: 20th Century Fox/Lucasfilm Ltd. Cast: Ewan McGregor (Obi-Wan "Ben" Kenobi), Liam Neeson (Jedi Master Qui Gon Jinn), Natalie Portman (Queen Padme)

The Rise and Fall of Little Voice/ AKA Little Voice UK 1998. 89 minutes. Director: Mark Herman. Screenplay: Jim Cartwright and Mark Herman, based on the play *The Rise and Fall of Little Voice* by Jim Cartwright. Production Company: Scala Productions. Cast: Jane Horrocks (Little Voice), Ewan McGregor (Billy), Michael Caine (Ray Say), Brenda Blethyn (Mother)

Rogue Trader UK 1998. tba minutes. Director: James Dearden. Screenplay: James Dearden, based on the autobiography *Rogue Trader* by Nick Leeson. Production Company: Granada Film Productions/Newmarket Capital. Cast: Ewan McGregor (Nick Leeson), Anna Friel (Lisa Leeson)

Eye of the Beholder USA 1998. tba minutes. Director: Stephan Elliot. Screenplay by Stephan Elliot, based on the novel by Marc Behm. Production Company: Filmline International Inc/Hit & Run Productions. Cast: Ewan McGregor (The Private Eye), Ashley Judd, Jason Priestley

FUTURE PROJECTS

South From Hell's Kitchen USA 1998. Director: Louis Nader. Production Company: Warner Brothers. Cast: Bridget Fonda, Ewan McGregor, Jean Rochefort

Nora UK 1999. Director: Pat Murphy. Screenplay: Pat Murphy. Production Company: Natural Nylon. Cast: Susan Lynch (Nora Barnacle), Ewan McGregor (James Joyce)

TELEVISION

Lipstick on Your Collar UK 1993. 180 minutes. Director: Renny Rye. Screenplay: Dennis Potter. Production Company: Whistling Gypsy Production/Channel Four Films. Cast: Louise Germaine (Sylvia Berry), Douglas Henshall

(Corporal Berry), Bernard Hill (Uncle Fred), Ewan McGregor (Private Mick Hopper)

Scarlet & Black UK 1993. 3 x 90 minutes. Director: Ben Bolt. Screenplay: Stephen Lowe based on the novel *Scarlet & Black* by Stendhal. Production Company: BBC. Cast: Ewan McGregor (Julien Sorel), Alice Krige, Stratford Johns, T.P. McKenna, Rachel Weisz

Doggin' Around UK 1994. 89 minutes. Director: Desmond Davis. Screenplay: Alan Plater. Production Company: Ariel Productions for the BBC. Cast: Elliot Gould (Joe Warren), Geraldine James (Sarah Williams), Ewan McGregor (Tom Clayton)

Kavanagh QC: "Nothing But The Truth" USA 1995. 90 minutes. Director: Paul Greengrass. Screenplay: Ted Childs. Production Company: Central Independent TV/Carlton UK. Cast: John Thaw (James Kavanagh QC), Geraldine James (Eleanor Harker QC), Ewan McGregor (David Armstrong), Alison Steadman (Eve Kendall)

Tales from The Crypt: "The Cold War" USA 1995. 60 minutes. Director: Andy Morahan. Production Company: Home Box Office (HBO). Cast: Ewan McGregor (Ford), Jane Horrocks (Ford's Girlfriend)

Karaoke UK 1996. 4 x 60 minutes. Director: Renny Rye. Screenplay: Dennis Potter. Production Company: Whistling Gypsy Production/(BBC)/ Channel Four Films. Cast: Hywel Bennett (Arthur 'Pig' Mallion), Albert Finney (Daniel Feeld) Richard E. Grant (Nick Balmer), Keeley Hawes (Linda Langer), Ewan McGregor (Young Man)

E.R.: "The Long Way Around" USA 1997. 60 minutes. Director: Christopher Chulak. Screenplay: Lydia Woodward. Production Company: Amblin Television/Constant c Productions/Warner Bros. TV. Cast: Ewan McGregor (Duncan Stewart), Julianna Margulies (Carol Hathaway, RN), George Clooney (Dr. Doug Ross)

SHORT FILMS

Family Style UK 1993. 15 minutes. Director: Justin Chadwick. Screenplay: Matthew Cooper. Production Company: Compulsive Viewing. Cast: Ewan McGregor (Jimmie), Amelia Curtis (Julie)

Swimming With the Fishes UK 1996. 30 minutes. Director: Justin Chadwick. Production Company: Compulsive Viewing. Cast: Ewan McGregor

THEATRE

What the Butler Saw Salisbury Playhouse 1993 Written by Joe Orton. Directed by Penny Cineiwicz. Cast: Ewan McGregor (Nick)

Little Malcolm and His Struggle Against the Eunuchs Hampstead Little Theatre, Hampstead Theatre Club 1998. Comedy Theatre, London, January 1999. Written by David Halliwell. Director: Denis Lawson. Cast: Ewan McGregor (Malcolm)